WHY READ AND STUDY DANIEL AND REVELATION?

Seven-headed dragons. Beasts rising up from the sea. Cryptic numbers like 666. Riddles like "MENE, MENE, TEKEL, PARSIN." What's going on in the books of Daniel and Revelation?

Maybe you've tried to read these books, but you gave up because they seemed so bizarre and difficult to understand. Maybe someone promised to show you from them what's going to happen at the end of the world, but then spun out a scenario that was too arbitrary and fanciful to believe. Experiences like these make many people avoid these books.

And that's a real shame, because they have a powerful message to share about how God is in control of history, and how no power on earth can defeat his purposes. Daniel and Revelation describe some of the most difficult experiences that people who love God have ever endured, and show how these people stayed loyal to him, even to the death. These books give us a glimpse into the never-ending worship that surrounds God in heaven and extends through all of creation. All of this is simply too good to miss.

And so we should read and study Daniel and Revelation. But we should do this responsibly, grounding these books in the times and places where they were written, appreciating the situations they were originally addressing, and understanding them as the special kind of writing they are. That's what this study guide will help you do. This is how we approach every other book of the Bible, and there's no reason to make these two books an exception.

When we read and study Daniel and Revelation this way, their story comes alive for us. They're not end-of-the-world speculation, but accounts of real people, in real-world situations, living out their faith with integrity instead of watering it down under pressure. Sure, these books can also help us understand what things may be like in the ultimate conflict between good and evil at the end of human history. But we don't have to wait until then to become part of the story they're telling. God needs people today who will suffer and sacrifice and worship and triumph just as the people in these two books do. Are you in?

UNDERSTANDING THE
BOOKS OF THE BIBLE

DANIEL
and
REVELATION

Also available in the
UNDERSTANDING THE BOOKS OF THE BIBLE series:

John
Genesis
Wisdom: Proverbs/Ecclesiastes/James
Joshua/Judges/Ruth—March 2011
Thessalonians/Corinthians/Galatians/Romans—March 2011

Future releases:

Exodus/Leviticus/Numbers
New Covenants: Deuteronomy/Hebrews
Samuel–Kings

Amos/Hosea/Micah/Isaiah
Zephaniah/Nahum/Habakkuk
Jeremiah/Obadiah/Ezekiel
Haggai/Zechariah/Jonah/Joel/Malachi

Psalms Books 1–3
Psalms Books 4–5/Song of Songs/Lamentations
Job
Chronicles/Ezra/Nehemiah/Esther

Matthew
Mark
Luke–Acts

Colossians/Ephesians/Philemon/Philippians/Timothy/Titus
Peter/Jude/John

UNDERSTANDING THE BOOKS OF THE BIBLE

DANIEL
and
REVELATION

Christopher R. Smith

Biblica™   Transforming lives through God's Word

Transforming lives through God's Word

Biblica provides God's Word to people through translation, publishing and Bible engagement in Africa, Asia Pacific, Europe, Latin American, Middle East, and North America. Through its worldwide reach, Biblica engages people with God's Word so that their lives are transformed through a relationship with Jesus Christ.

Biblica Publishing
We welcome your questions and comments.

1820 Jet Stream Drive, Colorado Springs, CO 80921 USA
www.Biblica.com

Understanding the Books of the Bible: Daniel/Revelation
ISBN-13: 978-1-60657-057-9

Copyright © 2011 by Christopher R. Smith

13 12 11 / 6 5 4 3 2 1

Published in 2011 by Biblica, Inc.™

A catalog record for this book is available through the Library of Congress.

Printed in the United States of America

CONTENTS

HOW THESE STUDY GUIDES ARE DIFFERENT

Did you know you could read and study the Bible without using any chapters or verses? The books of the Bible are real "books." They're meant to be experienced the same way other books are: as exciting, interesting works that keep you turning pages right to the end and then make you want to go back and savor each part. The UNDERSTANDING THE BOOKS OF THE BIBLE series of study guides will help you do that with the Bible.

While you can use these guides with any version or translation, they're especially designed to be used with *The Books of The Bible*, an edition of the Scriptures from Biblica that takes out the chapter and verse numbers and presents the biblical books in their natural form. Here's what people are saying about reading the Bible this way:

> I love it. I find myself understanding Scripture in a new way, with a fresh lens, and I feel spiritually refreshed as a result. I learn much more through stories being told, and with this new format, I feel the truth of the story come alive for me.

> Reading Scripture this way flows beautifully. I don't miss the chapter and verse numbers. I like them gone. They got in the way.

> I've been a reader of the Bible all of my life. But after reading just a few pages without chapters and verses, I was amazed at what I'd been missing all these years.

For more information about *The Books of The Bible* or to obtain a low-cost copy, visit http://www.thebooksofthebible.info. Premium editions of this Bible will be available in Spring 2011 from Zondervan at your favorite Christian retailer.

For people who are used to chapters and verses, reading and studying the Bible without them may take a little getting used to. It's like when you get a new cell phone or upgrade the operating system on your computer. You have to unlearn some old ways of doing things and learn some new ways. But it's not too long until you catch on to how the new system works and you find you can do a lot of things you couldn't do before.

Here are some of the ways you and your group will have a better experience of the Scriptures by using these study guides.

YOU'LL FOLLOW THE NATURAL FLOW OF BIBLICAL BOOKS

This guide will take you through the books of Daniel and Revelation following their natural flow. (The way these books unfold is illustrated in the outlines on pages 10 and 71.) You won't go chapter-by-chapter through either book, because chapter divisions in the Bible often come at the wrong places and break up the flow. (The divisions in the book of Daniel are better placed, however.) Did you know that the chapter divisions used in most modern Bibles were added more than a thousand years after the biblical books were written? And that the verse numbers were added more than three centuries after that? If you grew up with the chapter-and-verse system, it may feel like part of the inspired Word of God. But it's not. Those little numbers aren't holy, and when you read and study Daniel and Revelation without them, you'll hear the story emerge as never before.

To help you get a feel for where you are in each book's natural flow, the study sessions in this guide will be headed by a visual cue, like this:

Book of Daniel > Visions > Second Vision

YOU'LL UNDERSTAND WHOLE BOOKS

Imagine going to a friend's house to watch a movie you've never seen before. After only a couple of scenes, your friend stops the film and says, "So, tell me what you think of it so far." When you give your best shot at a reply, based on the little you've seen, your friend says, "You know, there's a scene in another movie that always makes me think of this one." He switches to a different movie and before you know it, you're watching a scene from the middle of another film.

Who would ever try to watch a movie this way? Yet many Bible studies take this approach to the Bible. They have you read a few paragraphs from one book of the Bible, then jump to a passage in another book. The UNDERSTANDING THE BOOKS OF THE BIBLE series doesn't do that. Instead, these study guides focus on understanding the message and meaning of one book at a time. This guide will make limited references to other biblical books only when Daniel or Revelation themselves allude to them.

Your group will read through the entire books of Daniel and Revelation, not just selected chapters or verses. Two of the sessions (session 1 and session 12) are overviews that let you experience these books as a whole, to prepare you for considering their individual sections. Reading through an entire book at once will be like viewing a whole movie before zooming in on one scene.

Groups that read books of the Bible aloud together have a great experience doing this. (If you've never done it before, give it a try—you'll be surprised at how well it flows and how fast the time passes.) For these overview sessions, the discussion will be briefer and designed to allow people to share their overall impressions.

YOU'LL DECIDE FOR YOURSELVES WHAT TO DISCUSS

In each session of this study guide there are many options for discussion. While each session could be completed by a group in about an hour and a half, any one of the questions could lead to an involved conversation. There's no need to cut the conversation short to try to "get through it all." As a group leader, you can read through all the questions ahead of time and decide which one(s) to begin with, and what order to take them up in. If you do get into an involved discussion of one question, you can leave out some of the others, or you can extend the study over more than one meeting if you do want to cover all of them.

TOGETHER, YOU'LL TELL THE STORY

Each session gives creative suggestions for reading the passage you'll be discussing. The guide will often invite the group to dramatize the Scriptures by reading them out loud like a play. The discussion options may also invite group members to retell the biblical story from a fresh perspective. This kind of telling and retelling is a spiritual discipline, similar to Bible memorization, that allows people to personalize the Scriptures and take them to heart. Our culture increasingly appreciates the value and authority of story, so this is a great discipline for us to cultivate.

If you're using *The Books of The Bible*, you'll find that the natural sections it marks off by white space match up with the sections of the reading. If you're using another edition of the Bible, you'll be able to identify these sections easily because they'll be indicated in this guide by their opening lines, or by some other means that makes them obvious.

EVERYONE WILL PARTICIPATE

There's plenty of opportunity for everyone in the group to participate. Because Daniel especially is a story with characters, as you read from it in each session, you'll often have different group members taking the parts of different characters. The readings in Revelation will also involve different people in various ways. Group members can read the session introduction aloud or the discussion questions as well. As a leader, you can easily involve quiet people by giving them these opportunities. And everyone will feel that they can speak up and answer the questions, because the questions aren't looking for "right answers." Instead, they invite the group to work together to understand the Bible.

YOU'LL ALL SHARE DEEPLY

The discussion questions will invite you to share deeply about your ideas and experiences. The answers to these questions can't be found just by "looking them up." They require reflection on the meaning of each whole passage, in the wider context of the book it belongs to, in light of your personal experience. These aren't the kind of abstract, academic questions that make the discussion feel like a test. Instead, they'll connect the Bible passage to your life in practical, personal, relational ways.

To create a climate of trust where this kind of deep sharing is encouraged, here are a couple of ground rules that your group should agree to at its first meeting:

- *Confidentiality.* Group members agree to keep what is shared in the group strictly confidential. "What's said in the group stays in the group."
- *Respect.* Group members will treat other members with respect at all times, even when disagreeing over ideas.

HOW TO LEAD GROUP STUDIES USING THIS GUIDE

Each session has three basic parts:

Introduction to the Study

Have a member of your group read the introduction to the session out loud to everyone. Then give group members the chance to ask questions about the introduction and offer their own thoughts and examples.

Reading from Daniel or Revelation

Read the selection out loud together. (The study guide will offer suggestions for various ways you can do this for each session. For example, sometimes you will assign different characters in the story to different readers, and sometimes different people will read different sections of the passage.)

Discussion Questions

Most questions are introduced with some observations. These may give some background to the history and culture of the ancient world or explain where you are in the flow of the story. After the observations there are suggested discussion questions. Many of them have multiple parts that are really just different ways of getting at an issue.

You don't have to discuss the questions in the order they appear in the study guide. You can choose to spend your time exploring just one or two questions and not do the others. Or you can have a shorter discussion of each question so that you do cover all of them. As the group leader, before the meeting you should read the questions and the observations that introduce them, and decide which ones you want to emphasize.

When you get to a given question, have someone read aloud the observations and the question. As you answer the question, interact with the observations (you can agree or disagree with them) in light of your reading from the Bible. Use only part of the question to get at the issue from one angle, or use all of the parts, as you choose.

Sometimes there will be things to do or think about in preparation for your next session. But there's never any "homework" in the traditional sense. Whenever a session ends with a section called "For Your Next Meeting," have someone read this information aloud to the group to explain how people should prepare for the next study.

TIPS FOR HOME GROUPS, SUNDAY SCHOOL CLASSES, COMMUNITY BIBLE EXPERIENCES, AND INDIVIDUAL USE

If you're using this guide in a *home group*, you may want to begin each meeting (or at least some meetings) by having dinner together. You may also want to have a time of singing and prayer before or after the study.

If you're using this guide in a *Sunday school class*, you may want to have a time of singing and prayer before or after the study.

This study guide can also be used in connection with a *community Bible experience* of the books of Daniel and Revelation. If you're using it in this way:

- Encourage people to read each session's Scripture passage by themselves early in the week (except for sessions 1 and 12, when the whole church will gather to hear these books read out loud).
- Do each session in midweek small groups.
- Invite people to write/create some response to each small-group session that could be shared in worship that weekend. These might involve poetry, journal or blog entries, artwork, dramas, videos, and so on. (The visions in Daniel and Revelation should provide a lot of great material for artists to work with!)
- During the weekend worship services, let people share these responses, and have preaching on the Scripture passage that was studied that week. Speakers can gather up comments they've heard from people and draw on their own reflections to sum up the church's experience of that passage.

This guide can also be used for *individual study*. You can write out your responses to the questions in a notebook or journal. (However, we really encourage reading and studying the Bible in community!)

DANIEL

OUTLINE OF THE BOOK OF DANIEL:
"WHAT HAPPENS WHEN"
Numbers correspond to sessions in this study guide

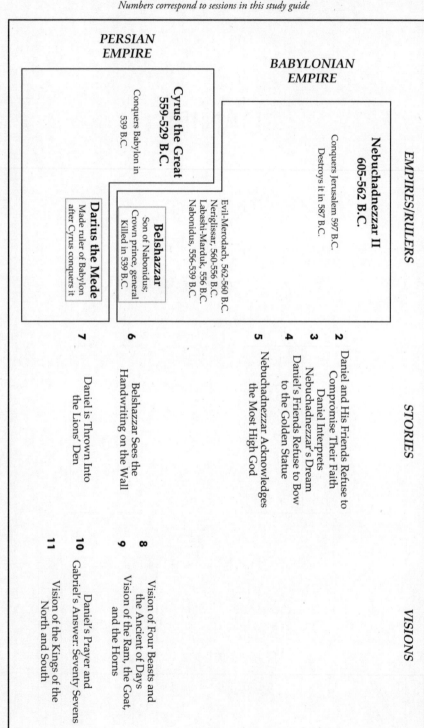

EMPIRES/RULERS	STORIES	VISIONS
BABYLONIAN EMPIRE		
Nebuchadnezzar II 605-562 B.C. Conquers Jerusalem 597 B.C. Destroys it in 587 B.C.	**2** Daniel and His Friends Refuse to Compromise Their Faith	
	3 Nebuchadnezzar's Dream Daniel Interprets	
	4 Daniel's Friends Refuse to Bow to the Golden Statue	
Evil-Merodach, 562-560 B.C. Neriglissar, 560-556 B.C. Labashi-Marduk, 556 B.C. Nabonidus, 556-559 B.C.	**5** Nebuchadnezzar Acknowledges the Most High God	
Belshazzar Son of Nabonidus; Crown prince, general Killed in 539 B.C.	**6** Belshazzar Sees the Handwriting on the Wall	**8** Vision of Four Beasts and the Ancient of Days
		9 Vision of the Ram, the Goat, and the Horns
PERSIAN EMPIRE		
Cyrus the Great 559-529 B.C. Conquers Babylon in 539 B.C.		
Darius the Mede Made ruler of Babylon after Cyrus conquers it	**7** Daniel is Thrown Into the Lions' Den	**10** Daniel's Prayer and Gabriel's Answer: Seventy Sevens
		11 Vision of the Kings of the North and South

GREAT EMPIRES IN DANIEL'S TIME

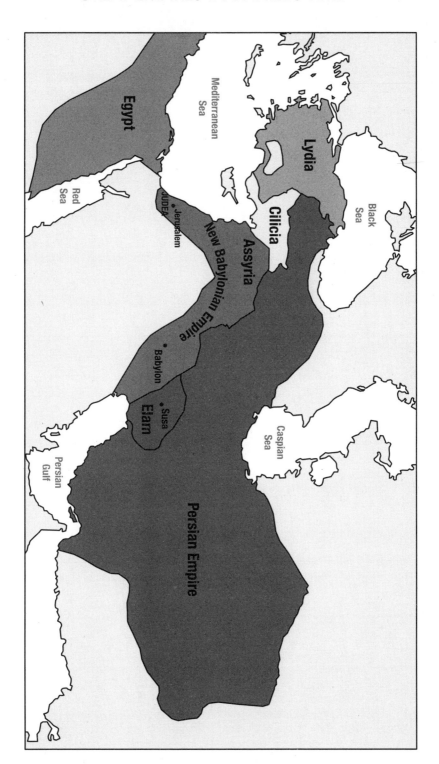

Egypt

Mediterranean Sea

Lydia

Cilicia

Black Sea

Red Sea

JUDEA

• Jerusalem

New Babylonian Empire

Assyria

• Babylon

Elam

• Susa

Caspian Sea

Persian Gulf

Persian Empire

EXPERIENCING THE BOOK OF DANIEL AS A WHOLE

INTRODUCTION

(Have someone read this introduction aloud for the rest of the group.)

Before considering the individual parts of any creative work, it's important to experience it as a whole. This gives you the "big picture," the overall message, and allows you to understand where each part fits. So in this session your group will begin its study of Daniel by reading the whole book aloud.

As you listen to the book of Daniel, you'll recognize that it has two main parts. The first part tells six stories of how God protected Daniel and his three friends, who were carried away as prisoners when the Babylonian empire conquered the kingdom of Judah shortly after 600 BC. (Notice how each story begins by describing something a king did that set the events of the story in motion.) Daniel and his friends resolved to remain faithful to God and not worship the gods of Babylon, no matter what it cost them. God rewarded their loyalty by preserving their lives in high-stakes situations where they could show that their God was the true ruler of all the "kingdoms on earth."

The second part of the book records four experiences that Daniel had later in his life when God communicated with him in extraordinary ways, through visions or angel messengers. God showed Daniel how history would unfold in the years ahead, because God wanted to warn his future followers that another time would come when they would have to take a strong stand against any religious compromise.

We'll look at these stories and visions in more detail in the following sessions. In this session, listen to how the book of Daniel unfolds and look for the major themes it develops.

READING

Have the members of your group take turns as you read through the book of Daniel out loud. It's on pages 1393–1410 in *The Books of The Bible*. If you're using another edition of the Scriptures, you can find Daniel in its table of contents.

If you have a copy of *The Books of The Bible*, begin by reading the introduction to Daniel on pages 1391–92. If you don't, the material on "Why Read and Study Daniel and Revelation?" at the beginning of this study guide will give you a basic sense of what the book is about. The outline on page 10 of this guide and the introductions to several of the following sessions will help you understand more about its major themes and style of writing.

It should only take about an hour to read through the book. You can have different people each read a whole story or vision report. (In *The Books of The Bible*, two blank lines mark the end of each story or vision. In the book of Daniel, the traditional chapters correspond pretty well with these natural divisions, so if you're not using *The Books of The Bible*, in this case you can rely on those chapters. However, the last vision includes chapters 10—12.) If people would prefer to read shorter sections, you can change readers whenever you feel you've come to a natural break in the story.

When it's your turn to read, think of yourself as telling the story to the rest of the group. If you prefer not to read aloud, just let the next person take their turn.

As you hear the book read, you can find locations like Judah, Jerusalem, Babylon, and Persia on the map and see where the action is taking place. You can follow the outline to see how the book is unfolding. Listen for how the major themes are being developed.

Note: When groups "tell the story" of a whole biblical book this way, they have a great experience together, so this is the approach we recommend.

DISCUSSION

⮑ What was it like to hear an entire book of the Bible read out loud?

⮑ What things struck you most as you listened? What were your overall impressions?

⮑ What would you say are the major themes or "big ideas" that the book of Daniel develops?

*STORIES OF DANIEL AND HIS
FRIENDS IN EXILE*

DANIEL AND HIS FRIENDS REFUSE TO COMPROMISE THEIR FAITH

Book of Daniel > Stories > First Story

INTRODUCTION

One of the places where human civilization first developed was in Mesopotamia, the area between the Tigris and Euphrates Rivers (part of modern-day Iraq). The city of Babylon was established in this area, and it long had a dominant cultural and military influence. After an earlier empire of theirs declined, the Babylonians spent several centuries under Assyrian rule, but in 626 BC they rebelled, and through a series of conquests in the following decades under the leadership of Nebuchadnezzar, they built one of the greatest empires of the ancient world. (See the map on page 11.)

Whenever the Babylonians conquered another kingdom, they carried away its educated ruling class to help staff the extensive bureaucracy they needed to govern their empire. (Depriving conquered peoples of their leaders also helped prevent rebellions.) A captive who adapted to the Babylonians' customs and learned their culture might be given a position of considerable importance.

As the book of Daniel opens, four captives from Judah are being given this opportunity. (Judah was one of two kingdoms that ancient Israel was divided into.) These are young men of strong faith who are deeply loyal to their God. How much religious compromise will be asked of them as they train to serve the Babylonian empire? Will they sacrifice their faith if they think their careers, and perhaps their lives, are at risk?

READING

This opening story in the book of Daniel begins by describing three serious challenges these Judean captives are facing:

- Their God appears to be defeated and humiliated: Articles from his temple have been put in the "trophy case" of the Babylonian god!
- They need to succeed in a difficult and competitive training program in order to work in the Babylonian government. Otherwise, they may become slaves.
- This program requires them to compromise what they believe is an essential aspect of their religious devotion: their kosher diet.

After describing these three challenges, this story explains how the challenges of the diet and the training program were met. The rest of the stories in Daniel describe how the first challenge was met—restoring God's reputation.

Have five people read the following parts of this story aloud:

 The challenge of God's apparent defeat. (beginning, "In the third year of the reign of Jehoiakim . . .").

 The challenge of the training program. ("Then the king ordered Ashpenaz . . .")

 The challenge of religious compromise. ("But Daniel resolved not to defile himself . . .")

 The outcome of Daniel's attempt to resist compromise. ("At the end of the ten days . . .")

The results of the training program. (beginning, "At the end of the time set by the king . . ." and reading through to the end of the story).

DISCUSSION

1 Daniel and his friends had to decide how much of the Babylonian culture they could adopt without fatally compromising their faith. They didn't take an all-or-nothing approach. They didn't say, "You've got to go along if you want to get along," and agree to everything the Babylonians expected. They also didn't say that everything Babylonian was evil and had to be rejected. They diligently studied the "language and literature of the Babylonians," even though this literature centered around the exploits of foreign gods. They also accepted new names that praised these gods instead of their own God:

- Daniel ("God is my judge/vindicator") became Belteshazzar (a name that invoked the Babylonian god Bel);
- Hananiah ("Yahweh is gracious") became Shadrach ("companion of Aku");
- Mishael ("Who is like God?") became Meshach (again invoking Aku); and
- Azariah ("Yahweh is my help") became Abednego ("servant of Nebo").

Somehow these young men determined that what they were studying, and the new names they were given, didn't compromise the essentials of their faith. But they drew the line when it came to eating foods that God had told the Israelites, in the law of Moses, not to eat, because they had a distinct identity as his people.

⊃ What kinds of situations might a person encounter today that would challenge them to compromise their values and beliefs? How can a person know where to draw the line in these situations, so that they cooperate where possible but never compromise essentials?

⮕ Could people's individual convictions legitimately differ, even if they arose from a shared set of beliefs or values, so that one person might be free to do something that another person couldn't? (For example, do you know some people who won't eat certain foods on religious grounds, and other people of the same religion who will eat those foods?) Are there things that no person of faith and integrity should ever do, even to get an influential position where they might do a lot of good?

2 Daniel doesn't refuse outright to eat the food he's been assigned. Instead, he explains his concerns to the chief official and the guard, and he ultimately works out a way to stay in the training program without compromising his convictions.

⮕ How does Daniel go about making his appeal so that it will be successful? (For example, he speaks with the official privately, rather than putting him on the spot in front of other people. What other effective approaches does he take? Some suggestions are given at the end of this study; you can interact with them once you've made your own list.)

⮕ Have you, or has someone you know, been able to appeal successfully to an authority the way Daniel does here? Share the story if you can.

3 This story tells us that "God gave knowledge and understanding" to these four young men, and that he gave Daniel the special ability to interpret visions and dreams. (This ability will prove crucial in the rest of the book.) The Judean captives do so well when they're examined at the end of the training period that they're taken into the "king's service" and begin to work as advisors in the Babylonian government.

⮕ What's the biggest learning challenge you've ever met successfully? (Speaking a new language, adapting to a disability, completing a job training program, getting a degree, etc.) What would you say were the most important things that helped you meet this challenge? If you believe that God helped you in some way, explain how.

NOTE

Suggested answer for section 2, question 1: Daniel helped his appeal to succeed by: first resolving firmly what outcome he had to work for; speaking privately with the official and guard; asking permission to try an alternative rather than outright refusing; understanding the authority's concern ("I'll get in trouble if you look less fit") and addressing that concern ("you can decide for yourself how we look"); offering a creative alternative and a trial period; not giving up after a first refusal, but not trying to go over the official's head, either—he made a second appeal to someone below him, within that person's more limited sphere of authority.

DANIEL INTERPRETS NEBUCHADNEZZAR'S DREAM

INTRODUCTION

By the end of the first story in the book of Daniel, the Judean captives have met two significant challenges. They've successfully completed a training program to serve in the Babylonian government, and they've been able to do this without compromising their faith. But a third challenge remains. Their God appears to have been unable to protect their country and even his own temple from being conquered and destroyed. But in the rest of the stories in this book, God will progressively reveal his wisdom, power, and supremacy over all the kingdoms of the earth.

God begins in this story by giving Nebuchadnezzar an inspired dream that discloses the general outlines of the future course of history. Nebuchadnezzar has been wondering what will happen to the empire he's built, so he's eager to know the dream's meaning. The only problem is, when he wakes up, he can't remember the dream itself . . .

READING

As a group, using your Bibles as a "script," act this story out like a play. (The narrator can leave out cues like "Then the astrologers answered the king,"

"The king replied to the astrologers," etc.) Make one place in your meeting room the king's court, another the astrologers' quarters in the palace, and another the house where Daniel and his friends live. The actors should move from place to place to illustrate the flow of the story.

(Note: Daniel's friends should go with him back to the king's court when he interprets the dream. The text suggests they were with him: Daniel says, "*we* will interpret it to the king," and Nebuchadnezzar uses the plural when he says, "*your* God is the God of gods.")

Have people take these parts:

> Narrator
> Nebuchadnezzar
> Astrologers
> Daniel
> Arioch
> Hananiah, Mishael, and Azariah (no spoken lines)

If you have enough actors, you can give three different people the three lines that the astrologers speak. If you don't have enough actors, you can have just one astrologer and not have anyone portray Daniel's friends.

When the narrator is reading and the actors aren't speaking, the actors should act out the events silently. For example, Daniel can mime for his friends at his house that he wants them to pray.

DISCUSSION

1 Nebuchadnezzar expects supernatural results from his religion. He asks all of his "magicians, enchanters, sorcerers and astrologers" to tell him a dream that he's forgotten. They protest that this request is "too difficult": "No king . . . has ever asked such a thing." This makes Nebuchadnezzar furious. He decides to execute them all. But Daniel declares that "there is a God in heaven who reveals mysteries" to human beings. When Daniel successfully relates the dream and explains its interpretation, Nebuchadnezzar acknowledges that Daniel's God is the "God of gods . . . and a revealer of mysteries."

⊃ Was Nebuchadnezzar right to want to "fire his religion" for not delivering supernatural results (by executing all of the "magicians, enchanters, sorcerers and astrologers")? Explain your view.

⊃ In his song of thanksgiving, Daniel says that "wisdom and power" belong to God, and that God has given them to him. If you've ever had an experience where you feel God has given you supernatural wisdom and power when you needed it, share this experience with the group.

2 Through Nebuchadnezzar's vivid dream, God revealed that there would be a succession of four empires in the Mesopotamian and Mediterranean world, followed by a kingdom that would "endure forever." The first of these empires is identified in the text: The statue's head of gold is the Babylonian empire. The chest of silver is the Persian empire, which conquered Babylon in 539 BC. (This event is described later in the book of Daniel.) History suggests that the belly of bronze is the empire of Alexander the Great. The prediction of a fourth empire seems to have had one fulfillment initially, and then a later, more definitive fulfillment (as biblical prophecies often do).

When Alexander the Great died, his empire was divided up among four of his generals. From the territory assigned to his general Seleucus, another great empire arose that in the following centuries grew to be almost as large as Alexander's original one. (See the maps on pages 26 and 27.)

In the second century BC, one of the rulers of this Seleucid empire desecrated the temple that had been restored in Jerusalem and tried to stamp out the worship of God. The Jews revolted, defeated the Seleucids, and restored their own independence and freedom of worship for nearly a century. This was the initial fulfillment of the prediction of a fourth empire and a kingdom that the "God of heaven will set up."

A further, more definitive fulfillment of this prediction can be recognized if the Seleucid empire is considered part of the belly of bronze and the fourth empire is understood as the Roman Empire instead. The kingdom that will "endure forever" would then be the "kingdom of heaven" that Jesus Christ declared was coming to earth starting with his own person and ministry.

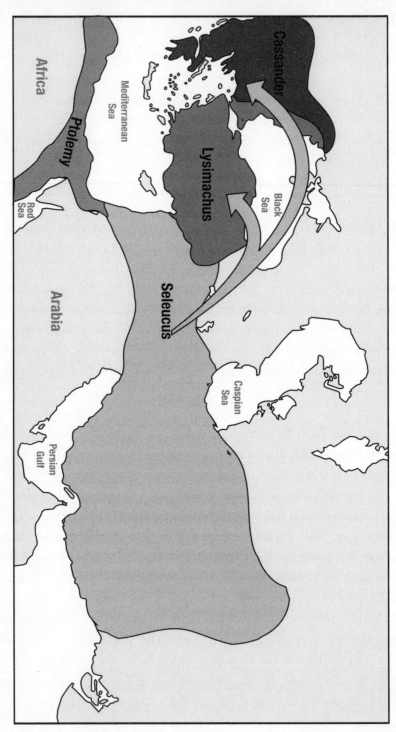

SELEUCID EMPIRE

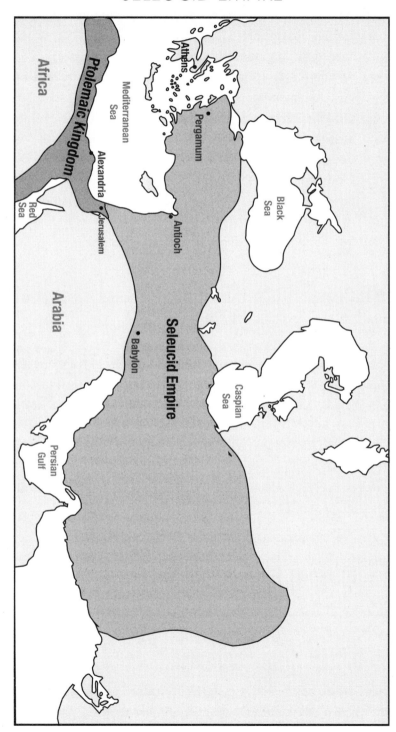

⮑ If God can show someone the future like this, does this mean that future events are predetermined and inevitable? Say which of the following explanations is closest to what you believe:

a. All future events are predetermined, and God can see and describe them because God is outside of time.

b. God has predetermined major events like the rise and fall of empires, but not smaller events within the big picture. These depend on the choices individuals make at the time.

c. God can predict the rough outlines of the future by knowing how people are likely to behave and extrapolating past trends forward.

d. Some other explanation. (What might that be?)

⮑ Does what a person believes about this make a difference in how they live their life? If so, how?

3 Nebuchadnezzar was wondering about the future of his empire. (Daniel notes, "As Your Majesty was lying there, your mind turned to things to come.") The take-home message of the dream is that his empire isn't going to last forever. In fact, in the foreseeable future it will be overrun by a rival empire. Daniel's task, as God's representative, is to challenge Nebuchadnezzar to accept this fact and humble himself before the "Lord of kings." This is the very same Nebuchadnezzar who decided to execute all of his advisors the last time they disappointed him!

⮑ Which of Daniel's experiences, in this story and in the previous one, do you think gave him the boldness to deliver this unwelcome interpretation exactly as God revealed it to him?

NOTE

You may have already heard the name Nebuchadnezzar, in the film series *The Matrix*, where it's the name of the hovercraft piloted by Morpheus. The film may be alluding to this story in the book of Daniel to suggest that the Matrix is a dream world whose true character most people are unable to understand.

FOR YOUR NEXT MEETING

To help you respond to question 1 next time, if you choose to, make sure there's a laptop available so that someone in your group who's good at writing can record and edit the group's response.

DANIEL'S FRIENDS REFUSE TO BOW TO THE GOLDEN STATUE

INTRODUCTION

God gave Nebuchadnezzar an inspired dream about a statue made of different materials. The interpretation was that the Babylonian empire (the statue's head of gold) wouldn't last forever; instead, it would ultimately be replaced by a kingdom that the "God of heaven" would set up. When Nebuchadnezzar first heard Daniel interpret his dream, he was so amazed that he "fell prostrate before" him and "paid him honor."

But now he's had a change of heart. He makes a statue entirely out of gold, to assert—in the language of the dream, and directly contradicting God's word—that his empire will last forever. He gathers provincial officials from all over his empire and demands that they "fall down" and "worship" this statue. (These are exactly the same Aramaic* words used to describe what Nebuchadnezzar did for Daniel; the king wants his empire to be on the receiving end this time!)

Daniel has gotten his friends Shadrach, Meshach, and Abednego appointed as provincial officials. This puts them in the crowd that's gathered before the statue and expected to bow down before it.

*The book of Daniel is written partly in Hebrew, the language of the people of Israel, and partly in Aramaic, the common language of the Babylonian empire. The Aramaic portion begins in the second story and ends after the first vision.

READING

Read this story out loud like a play. Have people read these parts:

    Narrator

    Herald

    Astrologers/advisers (choose one spokesperson for this group)

    Nebuchadnezzar

    Shadrach, Meshach, and Abednego (each actor can read one
       line in their part)

(As you read, you'll notice that this story contains many lists: of officials, musical instruments, articles of clothing, etc. This is a characteristic of oral storytelling. It shows that this story was first passed on by word of mouth before it was written down.)

DISCUSSION

1 Nebuchadnezzar leaves Daniel at the royal court (perhaps he doesn't feel ready to take him on directly) and sets up the statue on the plain of Dura, where he gathers all his provincial officials. This puts Shadrach, Meshach, and Abednego out where Daniel can't help or influence them.

> ⟳ Work together as a group to retell this story from the perspective of one of Daniel's three friends. (If there's a laptop available, have someone who's good at writing record and edit the story as the group develops it, and then read it when it's finished.) Tell the story in the first person (saying "I," "my," etc.). Begin when you're summoned out to the plain of Dura. When do you catch on to what's at stake? How do you reach your decision to disobey the king's command? How do you feel as the soldiers tie you up and carry you towards the furnace? What's it like to walk around in the flames with someone who "looks like a son of the gods"? As you look back over the experience, what will you remember most?

2 Shadrach, Meshach, and Abednego tell the king that if their God is able to deliver them, he will, but that even if he doesn't, they won't serve the Babylonian gods or worship the statue. Their obedience wasn't conditional on their deliverance. Nebuchadnezzar recognizes this and praises them for being "willing to give up their lives rather than serve or worship any god except their own God." (Does he wish he could command this kind of loyalty himself instead of having to threaten to kill people to get them to follow him?)

⮑ Sometimes God rescues his faithful followers from death, even through miraculous means like these. Can you tell the story of someone you know, or have heard about, who's been rescued like this? At other times people do have to give up their lives to remain loyal to God. Can you tell the story of someone who's done this? What do you think makes the difference—why does God rescue people sometimes, but not every time?

⮑ What do you think the officials would have told the people back in their provinces if Shadrach, Meshach, and Abednego hadn't been rescued, but instead gave their lives for their faith?

3 In Daniel's song of praise in the previous story, he said that "wisdom and power" belonged to God. When Daniel interpreted Nebuchadnezzar's dream, the king acknowledged God as a "revealer of mysteries"—a God of wisdom. Now he acknowledges that this God has "rescued his servants" and must also be a God of power. He forbids anyone in his empire to say anything against "the God of Shadrach, Meshach and Abednego."

⮑ On a scale of 1 to 10, with 1 being complete indifference or hostility to God, and 10 being lifelong commitment to serve and worship God, where would you say Nebuchadnezzar is at the end of this story? Where was he at the end of the previous story, and where was he at the beginning of this story?

⮑ Where would you place yourself on this same scale of 1 to 10? Where were you five years ago, and where do you think you'll be (or hope you'll be) five years from now?

NEBUCHADNEZZAR ACKNOWLEDGES THE MOST HIGH GOD

Book of Daniel > Stories > Fourth Story

INTRODUCTION

This story relates the climactic episode in God's dealings with Nebuchadnezzar. This king has previously recognized God's wisdom and power. But he still hasn't acknowledged God's sovereignty, that is, his authority over all the kingdoms of the earth. Nebuchadnezzar wants to believe that nothing is greater than the empire he's built—nothing can destroy it, and it will never end. (This was the symbolic message of the golden statue he made.) He needs to acknowledge that God's kingdom is the real "eternal dominion" that "endures from generation to generation."

READING

To reflect the significance of this climactic story, it's told in a form that the biblical writers considered beautiful and refined. The story is told in parts that are matched together. The first and last are paired, as are the second and next-to-last, and so forth. (A literary pattern built out of nested elements like this is known as a *chiasm*.)

A: Nebuchadnezzar begins his letter

  B: A song of praise to God

    C: Nebuchadnezzar tells his own story

      D: A narrator continues the story: Daniel's interpretation of the dream

(One year goes by)

      D: A narrator continues the story: Nebuchadnezzar's madness

    C: Nebuchadnezzar resumes his own story

  B: A song of praise to God

A: Nebuchadnezzar concludes his letter

Have four people read this story aloud for the rest of the group. Assign each person a letter from A to D and have them read the parts corresponding to those letters, with a brief pause in the middle of the story. Give these readers a moment to look over the text and recognize their parts from the different types of writing (letter, song, narrative) and the change in speakers (Nebuchadnezzar says "I," "my," etc.; the narrator says "he," "his," etc.). In *The Books of The Bible*, there's a slight break between each of these parts, and the songs of praise are presented as poetry. In most other editions of the Bible, these parts will each begin at the start of a new paragraph.

Catch the flow of this elegant pattern!

DISCUSSION

1 Since Nebuchadnezzar was able to overrun the kingdom of Judah and carry off the articles from the temple in Jerusalem, he probably concluded that the God who was worshipped there was just a tribal deity who was powerless before him and his imperial gods. But through vividly symbolic dreams and demonstrations of power, God has been working to show Nebuchadnezzar who he really is. God wants this king to know him and relate to him properly, by acknowledging his divine authority.

In this second dream, God speaks to Nebuchadnezzar in symbolic language reminiscent of the first dream. The king had been represented as the head of a giant statue; now he's depicted as a giant tree. Daniel told him, when interpreting the first dream, that God had placed in his hands "all people everywhere and the beasts of the field and the birds in the sky." In this second dream, the tree provides "food for all," "shelter to the wild animals" and "nesting places in its branches for the birds." And just as inferior kingdoms were represented by the bronze and iron parts of the statue, Nebuchadnezzar is now told that his splendor will be taken away from him and he'll be left as a stump "bound with iron and bronze" until he acknowledges the authority of the Most High.

⮑ Have you ever felt God was trying to tell you something? Share, if you're comfortable, what means you think God was using to communicate; what God was saying; and how you responded. Did God speak in a consistent way that helped you recognize his voice? Did someone help "interpret" what God was saying, as Daniel does here?

⮑ In order to relate more properly to God, do you need to think less of yourself, or more of yourself?

2 Nebuchadnezzar's pride is the main obstacle to his relationship with God. But it's also affecting the way he treats other people. Daniel tells him, "Renounce your sins by doing what is right, and your wickedness by being kind to the oppressed." This suggests that, as emperor, Nebuchadnezzar feels he can do whatever he wants, and he's been oppressing his subjects. We can infer that he does change his ways for a time, because nothing happens to him right away, even though a verdict has been announced against him. However, after a year, his pride gets the best of him, and the verdict is carried out. He experiences retributive justice: The one who put himself above other people is put below them. He thinks and acts like an animal. He even starts to look like one.

⮑ There's a fine line between pride in the positive sense (a healthy self-respect and self-acceptance, and a feeling of personal dignity) and pride in the negative sense (an arrogant superiority that poisons our relationships with God and other people). What are some of the danger signs that we're heading over the line into the negative side of pride? What are some good ways to cultivate humility, besides having to eat grass like an ox for seven years?

3 The take-home message of this story should *not* be that mental illness is a punishment from God. In this particular case, it was used as a judgment and a restraint on Nebuchadnezzar, but it was also a means that God used constructively in Nebuchadnezzar's life. He was alienated from God, himself, and other people when he was strutting around on the roof of his palace bragging about his "mighty power" and the "glory of my majesty." His relationships were restored when, through a haze of madness, he looked up to heaven and recognized his true place before God.

Mental illness has a wide range of causes that can be very difficult to identify. In some cases it can so destructive and oppressive that it must be seen as something evil to be opposed and overcome with every resource that God provides. But in other cases, when the mind departs from its usual range of functioning, it may be actually trying to help a person who's desperately working out a crucial life issue that they haven't been able to address in any other way. A person may ultimately benefit from the experience if they can go through it with the help and support of their family and friends. Parker Palmer writes in his book *Let Your Life Speak* that he was able to recover from a serious depression and move into a new, productive phase of life when a counselor encouraged him to look at the depression not as "the hand of an enemy trying to crush you" but as "the hand of a friend, pressing you to the ground on which it is safe to stand."

⮑ Pray together as a group for the healing and restoration of those who suffer from mental illnesses. If people feel comfortable, they can mention the first names of those they'd like the group to pray for individually.

BELSHAZZAR SEES THE HANDWRITING ON THE WALL

Book of Daniel > Stories > Fifth Story

INTRODUCTION

After receiving inspired dreams, seeing demonstrations of God's wisdom and power, and going through a deeply humbling experience, Nebuchadnezzar acknowledged God's authority. But his successor Belshazzar, despite knowing all about these experiences, is openly defiant of this same God. He takes the goblets from the temple in Jerusalem and uses them to pour out drink offerings to the gods of Babylon. He's desperate: Twenty years after Nebuchadnezzar's death, the Babylonian empire is crumbling before the invading Persians, just as the statue dream predicted. But instead of accepting God's purposes and seeing where he might fit within them, Belshazzar appeals to the Babylonian gods to keep him on the throne. God immediately sends a mysterious, terrifying message in response.

READING

Read this story out loud like a play. Have people take these parts:

Narrator	The queen
King Belshazzar	Daniel

Note: in this story, the term "father," applied to Nebuchadnezzar, means "ancestor" or "predecessor." "Son," applied to Belshazzar, means "descendant" or "successor." After Nebuchadnezzar died, three other kings ruled briefly, and then Belshazzar's father Nabonidus became emperor. Belshazzar is actually the viceroy of Babylon, sitting as "king" in his father's absence. (See the outline on page 10.) The "queen" may actually be the queen mother, Nebuchadnezzar's widow.

DISCUSSION

1 As in the case of Nebuchadnezzar's forgotten dream, the "wise men and enchanters" face a double challenge here. They first need to figure out what the inscription says, and then they have to interpret its meaning. Only Daniel, by God's power, can do this. He explains that the inscription is a play on words.

In one sense, it lists the names of three coins of decreasing value: the *minah* (worth many shekels), the *tekel* (the Aramaic form of the word *shekel* itself), and the *peres* (half-shekel; *parsin* is the plural). This duplicates the image in the statue dream of materials of decreasing value, underscoring God's purposes to replace the Babylonian empire with later ones. (The narrator echoes this image by describing how the goblets from Jerusalem were gold and silver, while the gods of Babylon were gold, silver, bronze, iron, wood, and stone.)

But the meaning of the inscription also rests on the derivation of the names of these coins. *Minah* comes from a verb meaning "to count" or "to number"; *tekel* comes from the verb "to weigh"; and *peres* from a verb meaning "to divide." Daniel explains how all of these meanings apply to Belshazzar and his doomed empire. (*Peres* is also a play on the word "Persian.")

⮑ Why doesn't God just send Daniel or another representative to tell Belshazzar in plain language that his empire is doomed? Why the scary hand, the inscription none of the advisors can read, the need for the queen mother's intervention, and the multiple meanings of the interpretation? Explain why God communicated with Belshazzar through these means.

2 After God spoke to Nebuchadnezzar through the statue dream, that king defied God's word by setting up a statue of pure gold, asserting that his empire would last forever. In the same way, when God speaks to Belshazzar, he defies God by rewarding Daniel with the powers and emblems of a high office in his empire, as if it weren't doomed. God continued to speak to Nebuchadnezzar and work in his life until he acknowledged him. But Belshazzar is killed this same night.

Have everyone answer these two questions individually, and then share their answers with the group.

⊃ Why do you think Belshazzar experienced immediate judgment, when Nebuchadnezzar got so many "second chances"? Was it because Belshazzar's defiance of God was so brazen? Did God see something different in his heart ("you have been weighed . . . and *found wanting*)? Did God expect Belshazzar to learn from what happened to his famous predecessor ("you . . . have not humbled yourself, *though you knew all this*")? Or is there some other explanation?

⊃ Based on the answer you gave to the previous question, describe one specific thing you can do to be more like Nebuchadnezzar (open to God's continuing work in your heart, even if you resist at times) and less like Belshazzar. For example, if you thought Belshazzar was expected to learn from Nebuchadnezzar's example, name one important lesson you will put into practice that you've learned from the experience of someone you've known or heard about.

NOTE

The popular phrase "seeing the handwriting on the wall" comes from this story. It means recognizing that an organization or enterprise you're part of is doomed, and that you'd better get out while you can. (Belshazzar never managed to "see the handwriting on the wall" in this sense!)

DANIEL IS THROWN INTO THE LIONS' DEN

Book of Daniel > Stories > Sixth Story

INTRODUCTION

Babylon has been overthrown by the armies of the Persian emperor Cyrus. He has appointed Darius to rule the former domain of the Babylonians within his empire. Darius sets up his administration, employing some experienced officials from the former regime, and he soon discovers that Daniel has exceptional qualities of leadership and integrity that will make him an ideal administrator of his domain. But jealous and dishonest rivals trick the king into signing an edict that Daniel must violate if he wants to keep worshipping God. This puts his influential position at risk, and his life in danger.

READING

Read this story out loud like a play. Have people take these parts:
Narrator
Administrators and satraps (three or four people can share this
part and take turns speaking the lines)
King Darius
Daniel

If your group has younger children who usually do a different activity during your meeting, they can stay with the adults for this reading. Have them roar menacingly every time they hear the phrase, "the lion's den."

DISCUSSION

1 Like Shadrach, Meshach, and Abednego, Daniel is willing to die for his faith if God doesn't deliver him from a deadly penalty. But Daniel could have avoided this penalty much more easily. His three friends had to refuse publicly to bow down to an idol. Daniel, however, could simply have prayed privately and silently for a month to maintain his devotional practices, and stayed out of trouble.

➲ Why do you think Daniel considered it so important to continue his open, public devotion to God? Besides having a private personal faith, what public expressions of devotion (such as going to church, being baptized, listing a religious commitment on your Facebook page, etc.) do you think are essential? Why?

2 When Daniel first refused to compromise his faith, he was a young prisoner of war with much less to lose. Now that he could rule the entire realm where he was taken as a captive, he still considers his faith more important.

➲ Have a younger adult member of your group "interview" several of the older members (with everyone else listening) and ask them if certain aspects of their faith have been more challenging to maintain publicly as their lives have changed over the years. Do they now feel they have more to lose than when they were younger? What advice would they give about how to remain faithful all through life?

3 Most of the king's other officials were dishonest, even though they were supposed to make sure that the king didn't "suffer loss" from embezzlement. They didn't want an honest person in charge of them who would discover and report their thefts. Dishonest people know, from personal experience, right where to look in another person's life to find "corruption" and "grounds for charges." If they can't find any, as they couldn't for Daniel, they're prepared to lie and cheat to get rid of an honest person. They tell the king that his officials "have *all* agreed" he should pass an edict forbidding prayer. This makes Darius believe that Daniel has agreed to this, too, and he accepts their plan. Dishonest people also recognize a person of integrity, who can't be compromised, when they see one. These officials had no contingency plan, no other way to trap Daniel, if he decided not to pray. They didn't need one. They knew what he would do.

⊃ Imagine yourself, perhaps some years in the future, about to move into a position of influence where you can put your faith to work to make a difference in the world. People who don't want you to do this go looking for "skeletons in your closet"—evidence of cheating, corruption, or negligence they can use to disqualify you. Will they find anything? Are there areas of your life you can make changes in now so that when this time comes, there will be no "grounds for charges"? Look for a trustworthy accountability partner you can speak with in complete confidentiality about the changes you want to make, and ask this person to pray for you and check in with you regularly about your progress.

⊃ Daniel's life illustrates a principle that Jesus explained to his followers: The one who is faithful in small things will be faithful in big things. As we've seen in the stories in this book, Daniel built a pattern of faithfulness to God into his life starting when he was young. It stayed with him as he grew older and moved into higher positions of greater influence. What "small thing" could you start with today in order to begin building a pattern of faithfulness into your own life?

4 Like Nebuchadnezzar before him, Darius sees a demonstration of God's power, and he makes a proclamation to his whole kingdom about this God who "performs signs and wonders." But Darius is also very impressed, as Nebuchadnezzar was, by how devoted this God's servants are to him. Nebuchadnezzar praised "the God of Shadrach, Meshach and Abednego," who were "willing to give up their lives rather than serve or worship any god except their own God." And Darius notes twice how Daniel serves God "continually"—no matter what the obstacle or cost.

Deliverance from a fiery furnace or den of lions is exceptional and miraculous. As we noted in an earlier session, God can and does still sometimes deliver his followers from deadly peril, although at other times it's their faithfulness to the death that provides a powerful testimony. Beyond such life-and-death situations, a person's continual devotion to God, through all of life's struggles and trials and challenges, speaks eloquently of how much a relationship with God is worth.

⮑ Do you know someone whose constant loyalty to God is an inspiration to you? Share their story with the group if you can.

FOR YOUR NEXT MEETING

Make sure that the group has internet access, if possible, to watch a seven-minute worship video at the end of your discussion time.

DANIEL'S VISIONS
OF THE FUTURE

DANIEL'S VISION OF FOUR BEASTS AND THE ANCIENT OF DAYS

Book of Daniel > Visions > First Vision

INTRODUCTION

We now come to a significant transition in the book of Daniel. As we move from the series of stories into the series of visions, the type of writing changes: It's no longer narrative, but apocalypse.

The word *apocalypse* is often used to mean an end-of-the-world disaster (as in the film title *Apocalypse Now*, or the *Sports Illustrated* feature "Sign of the Apocalypse"). But the word actually means an "unveiling." In apocalypses, a type of writing that flourished in the ancient world for several hundred years, a messenger sent from God "lifts the veil" and reveals the secrets of the future and of the heavenly realm. The person who's given this revelation describes how they received it, speaking in the first person (saying "I," "my," etc.). This will be the pattern in the rest of the book of Daniel.

There's another significant transition here, a thematic one. Up to this point in the book, it's been possible for Daniel and his friends to serve God faithfully in a foreign court. When they've had to stand their ground in a direct confrontation, God has delivered them miraculously. But these visions warn that in the days to come, things will change. God's people will be persecuted and killed. Evil will not prevail in the end, but until their deliverance comes, the "holy people of the Most High" need to be prepared to suffer and sacrifice

ANCIENT EMPIRES DEPICTED IN DREAMS AND VISIONS IN THE BOOK OF DANIEL

EMPIRE	STATUE DREAM	VISION OF FOUR BEASTS	RAM/GOAT VISION
Babylonian	Head of gold	**Lion** • Losing eagle wings, standing upright alludes to Nebuchadnezzar's recovery from madness	
Persian	Chest of silver	**Bear** • "Raised up on one of its sides" because Persians were more powerful • Devouring three ribs = conquests of Babylon, Lydia, and Egypt	**Ram** • The "later" horn was "higher"; Persians became more powerful • West, north, south: conquests of Babylon, Lydia, Egypt
Greek (Alexander the Great)	Belly of bronze	**Leopard** • 4 wings = speed of conquest • 4 heads = division among 4 generals after Alexander dies	**Goat** • prominent horn = Alexander • not touching the ground = speed of conquest • 4 horns = division of empire among 4 generals after Alexander dies
Seleucid	**Legs of iron** • may also represent the Roman Empire in a later fulfillment of this dream	**Frightening beast** • 10 horns = 10 kings who ruled Seleucid empire after Alexander starting with general Seleucus • 3 uprooted horns = 3 kings or heirs who were murdered or deposed so that Antiochus IV became emperor • "Little horn" that can see and speak = Antiochus's pretensions to divinity	**Little Horn** • Seleucid emperor Antiochus IV "Epiphanes," 175–64 BC • grew "to the south and to the east and toward the Beautiful Land" = Antiochus campaigns in Egypt, Persia, Palestine • Throwing down starry host, challenging the LORD's commander = Antiochus's pretensions to divinity

for their faith, rather than make any compromise. This theme is introduced in the first vision in the book of Daniel.

READING

Have one person read aloud Daniel's description of his vision of four beasts coming up from the sea.

Then have another person read the interpretation of the vision (beginning, "I, Daniel, was troubled in spirit . . .").

DISCUSSION

1 In the visions described in apocalypses, animals often represent people or nations. That's how the symbolism works here. The interpreter explains to Daniel, "the four great beasts are four kings"; "the fourth beast is a fourth kingdom." These four empires are the same ones envisioned in Nebuchadnezzar's dream about the statue.

➲ Look together at the third column of the chart on page 47, which shows how this vision relates to the statue dream and offers an interpretation of many of its details. Discuss the interpretation together and let people ask any questions they want about it. It may be helpful to re-read the explanation of Nebuchadnezzar's dream provided in question 2 of session 3, and to look again at the maps on pages 11, 26, and 27.

➲ Why do you think God communicated with Daniel through the complex imagery of these visions? What do you think is the purpose of this type of writing that we call apocalypse?

2 The main concern of this vision is the "little horn" that has human eyes and can speak. In apocalyptic visions, just as animals represent humans, humans often represent divine figures. So the ability to see (understand) and speak symbolizes this king's pretensions to divinity.

The person envisioned is most likely Antiochus IV, a Seleucid emperor who ruled from 175–164 BC. He gave himself the title "Epiphanes" to assert that he was a "manifestation of God" on earth. He conquered the rival Ptolemaic kingdom of Egypt (we'll hear much more about this rivalry in Session 11), but the Romans then deposed him from the Egyptian throne. Humiliated, Antiochus vented his fury on the Jews in Jerusalem and Judea (thus the vision predicts, "he will . . . oppress [the Most High's] holy people"). They were part of his empire, but had resisted his efforts to impose Greek culture and religion. So he burned their Scriptures and forbade them to practice circumcision or observe the Sabbath and annual festivals ("he will . . . change the set times and the laws").

This prompted a rebellion under the Maccabees that restored Jewish independence and freedom of worship. But this independence came only after a period of struggle and oppression ("a time, times and half a time," three and a half years) when many compromised their faith while others suffered and died for it. The vision Daniel received and recorded was designed to warn God's faithful people and prepare them to face this challenge.

Just as Nebuchadnezzar's dream about the statue had one immediate fulfillment and then a later, more definitive one, so the warning in this vision has applied to many later time periods, and it may have a final fulfillment in an ultimate conflict between good and evil at the end of this age of human history.

⊃ What places do you know about in the world today where people are being persecuted and killed for their faith? Are you personally acquainted with people from any of these places? If so, share what you know with rest of the group. Pray together for those who are suffering persecution, that God would comfort, strengthen, and deliver them.

⊃ Speculative scenarios are constantly being spun out that try to predict what will happen in the "end times." Much in these scenarios is based on reinterpretations of the visions in the book of Daniel. *Briefly* describe some of the scenarios you've heard over the years.

⊃ Speculative details aside, what fundamental lessons does this vision teach that can equip believers to take their part in the ongoing conflict between good and evil, whether or not they see the climax of this conflict at the end of this present age?

3 This vision culminates in a triumphant view of the "Ancient of Days" and the "Son of Man" who's presented before him. Throughout the book of Daniel, the question of dominion has been pursued: Ultimately, who rules? Supreme authority is described as extending over all space ("all the nations and peoples of every language in all the earth") and all time ("an everlasting dominion . . . that will never be destroyed"). The customary royal salutation, "O king, live forever," points to these aspirations. But as Nebuchadnezzar and Darius acknowledged, and as this vision now symbolizes, God is the one who truly "lives forever." That's what the Aramaic phrase "Ancient of Days" signifies. The implications are that God holds supreme authority.

We've seen that the convention in apocalypses is to use humans to represent divine figures. The person who's presented to the Ancient of Days here is described as "like a son of man." This Aramaic phrase means that he "looked like a human being," but the implications within the vision are that he was divine.

The Jewish people took the phrase "son of man" from this vision and used it as a title ("Son of Man") to describe the divine savior figure they were expecting. Jesus often applied this title to himself, both to show that he was the Savior sent from God, and also, paradoxically, to show that he had given up his divine prerogatives and come to earth humbly, in human form, to identify completely with those he came to save.

⊃ What praise songs, hymns or poems do you know that acknowledge God's supreme authority by using the title "Ancient of Days"? Which ones do you know that use the title "Son of Man" to acknowledge Jesus as the Savior sent by God who came as a human being? Quote them if you can, or if you have internet access, find the words by using a search engine.

➲ Conclude your time together, if you wish, by watching an online video of Ron Kenoly singing "Ancient of Days." (Go to http://www. youtube.com/watch?v=UOe5GpqFJrE, or search online if the video has moved.)

DANIEL'S VISION OF THE RAM, THE GOAT, AND THE HORNS

Book of Daniel > Visions > Second Vision

INTRODUCTION

A couple of years after his first vision, Daniel sees a second one that foretells some of the same events and provides further details about them. Daniel sees himself in the Persian capital of Susa. He has this vision in the year that Cyrus of Persia ceases to be a vassal of the Medes and becomes their partner in a campaign of conquest that will eventually topple Babylon. The "desolation" of Jerusalem could soon end. So the vision begins by focusing on some very hopeful developments. However, the vision goes on to warn that later in history a sinister figure, already depicted in the previous vision, will emerge and once again devastate Jewish life and worship.

READING

Have one person read Daniel's description of his vision of the ram, the goat, and the horns.

Then have another person read the interpretation of the vision (beginning, "While I, Daniel, was watching the vision and trying to understand it . . .").

(Note: when Gabriel addresses Daniel as "son of man," this means simply "human being.")

DISCUSSION

1 In this vision animals once again represent nations and their rulers. Gabriel explains that the ram represents "the kings of Media and Persia" and the goat represents Greece. Its large horn is "the first king" (Alexander the Great); the four horns that replace it are "four kingdoms that will emerge from his nation" (Alexander's empire divided among four of his generals). This vision, like the first one, then focuses on the Seleucid emperor Antiochus IV "Epiphanes." He's depicted once again as a "little horn" with pretensions to divinity. Another warning is given about how he will ruthlessly suppress worship in the Jerusalem temple.

⟳ Look together at the fourth column of the chart on page 47, which shows how this vision relates to earlier ones in Daniel and offers an interpretation of many of its details. Discuss the interpretation together and let people ask any questions about it. It may also be helpful to look again at the maps on pages 26 and 27.

2 This vision gives more details of how Antiochus will suppress Jewish worship in Jerusalem. It describes how he will take away "the daily sacrifice" at the restored temple. It also speaks of a "rebellion that causes desolation." (The next two visions in the book of Daniel call this an "abomination that causes desolation.") This is likely a reference to the way Antiochus desecrated the temple. He sacrificed a pig on the altar and tried to force the Jews to eat this forbidden food. He also set up an image of Zeus in the temple. These will be such horrifying outrages that a "holy one" who's also watching this vision asks how long the temple will remain desecrated. The answer is "2,300 evenings and mornings."

Many interpreters believe that an "evening and morning" means one day. In that case, the phrase describes the six-and-a-half-year period that Jewish religious life was under Antiochus's control, beginning when the high priest Jason made an alliance with him in 171 BC. Other interpreters believe that

"2,300 evenings and mornings" means 1,150 evenings paired with 1,150 mornings, or 1,150 days (a little over three years, equivalent to the "time, times and half a time" of Daniel's first vision). This would describe a period beginning with the actual desecration of the temple in 167 BC. Either way we understand the phrase, the time period it indicates ends in 164 BC when the Jews, after fighting off Antiochus and reclaiming their independence and freedom of worship, cleansed and rededicated the temple (an event still commemorated today in the festival of Hanukkah).

As we've already noted, however, biblical prophecies can have an initial fulfillment, and then one or more later ones. Jesus said, as he foretold the destruction of the Jerusalem temple by the Romans in 70 AD, that this would be a further fulfillment of Daniel's prediction of an "abomination that causes desolation." While this was another event that devastated Jewish life and worship, this second fulfillment did not involve an actual ritual desecration, and there was no correspondence with many of the other details in this vision.

In other words, the specific details relate most directly to the vision's initial fulfillment. Any future fulfillments, including one in the ultimate conflict between good and evil at the end of history, will involve events of a similar *character*, but not necessarily a reconstitution of all of the specific elements. Since the visions in the book of Daniel primarily describe events that have already taken place in the past, we don't need to scan the news trying to match their details with impending events. Instead, we can draw on their insights to equip us to take our place in the struggle against evil in our own day, however near or far away the "time of the end" may be.

⮑ Which of the following insights from this vision do you find most encouraging as you face the future yourself? Explain why to the group.

- This crisis didn't take God by surprise.
- This evil ruler's days in power were limited from the start.
- The challenge was overcome "not by human power" but by God.
- The community of God's people endured faithfully through this crisis.

- God sent warning and encouragement to his people ahead of time.
- (Some other insight you've gotten from the vision.)

DANIEL'S PRAYER AND GABRIEL'S ANSWER: SEVENTY SEVENS

Book of Daniel > Visions > Third Vision

INTRODUCTION

Gabriel appears to Daniel again in the "first year of Darius." The former Babylonian kingdom now has new rulers—the Persians. Their policy is to let people who were taken into exile by the Babylonians return to their homelands. Daniel wonders whether, under these favorable conditions, God will allow the Jews to return to Jerusalem and rebuild the temple. He searches the Scriptures (as they existed in his day) and discovers that Jeremiah predicted that the "desolation of Jerusalem" would last seventy years. It's been less than fifty years since Nebuchadnezzar destroyed the temple. Does this mean that the Jews will have to wait another twenty years in exile, even though they could return home right away? Or might God shorten the period of time that was announced in Jeremiah's prophecy? Daniel prays fervently for God to show mercy, and Gabriel brings an answer.

READING

Have someone read the introduction to Daniel's prayer.

As a group, read Daniel's prayer in unison (out loud all together).

Then have someone read the description of Gabriel's appearance to Daniel.

DISCUSSION

1 Daniel's prayer here is one of the longest recorded in the Bible, and it provides an excellent model for our own prayers. It effectively blends the elements of adoration, confession, and petition. It shows deep insight into the character and purposes of God and expresses a passion for God's reputation and glory. And, as we'll see in question 2, it got results.

⮑ Divide your group into four teams to investigate the following questions and then share the answers with the group as a whole:

- About what percentage of this prayer is made up of adoration? Of confession? Of petition? Why do you think Daniel put his prayer together this way?
- Daniel says he's making his request based not on what he and his nation deserve, but based on God's character. In what different ways does Daniel describe God's character in his prayer?
- What reasons does Daniel give why God should grant his request? (Why is it in God's interests?)
- How does the tone that Daniel takes with God change and develop over the course of the prayer? What words can you think of to describe his tone or stance at different points?

⮑ Let anyone who wishes describe one way they want this prayer to serve as a model for their own prayers.

2 In the "first year of Nebuchadnezzar king of Babylon" (605 BC), Jeremiah prophesied that this king would invade and conquer the kingdom of Judah and make it "a desolate wasteland" for "seventy years." A few years later God promised through Jeremiah that he would bring the people back "when seventy years are completed."

Nebuchadnezzar destroyed Jerusalem in 587 BC, and Daniel prayed his prayer in 539 BC. Based on Jeremiah's prophecy, he shouldn't have expected the people to be able to return for another 22 years. So what stirred this godly man with visionary insight to pray that God would "turn away his anger and wrath from Jerusalem" right away? And why did God answer this prayer? He brought the people back much sooner than Jeremiah predicted: The Judeans returned home the next year.

⮑ Do you agree or disagree with the following statement? Why?

> "God inspires prophets to announce his purposes as of a given moment, but God is always interacting 'live' with humanity, and God can fulfill those same purposes in whatever way he finds most appropriate in the future as the divine-human relationship unfolds. In particular, God is always free to show mercy and not carry out all of a judgment that has been announced."

3 Daniel called his earlier vision of the ram, goat, and horns "beyond understanding." Jerusalem was already "desolate" because the Babylonians had destroyed it. There was no worship or sacrifice in the temple—it had been reduced to rubble. So why did this vision say that Jerusalem would be *made* desolate and sacrifices *ended* at some time in the *future*? In response to Daniel's prayer, Gabriel appears to help him "understand the vision." He describes a period of "seventy 'sevens.'" (These "sevens" are usually understood as seven-year periods.)

Biblical scholars have discussed and debated Gabriel's words extensively, but they haven't reached any consensus about how to interpret them. It's not obvious how they line up with events in later history, and attempts to explain them can quickly become speculative and fanciful. One observation we can make, however, is that many of the details Gabriel provides seem to correspond with events in the reign of Antiochus IV Epiphanes:

• "The Anointed One will be put to death" may describe the murder of the Jewish high priest Onias by his rival Jason in 171 BC.

- "He will confirm a covenant with many" may refer to the agreement Antiochus made with the Jewish nation once Jason seized power.
- "In the middle of the 'seven' he will put an end to sacrifice and offering" may describe how Antiochus suppressed Jewish worship three-and-a-half years after making this agreement.
- "He will set up an abomination that causes desolation" may indicate how Antiochus desecrated the temple.
- "The end that is decreed is poured out on him" could describe Antiochus's sudden death from disease in 164 BC.

The explanation of what Daniel found "beyond understanding" in the previous vision, therefore, is that the temple, desolate in his day, will be rebuilt, but then desolated again by an evil ruler who will ultimately be judged by God. This is a further warning to God's people that they need to be faithful, even to death, and refuse any compromise. It's still not evident, however, how the "seventy 'sevens'" get the reader down to the time of Antiochus from Daniel's day. So, much remains to be understood in this fascinating but cryptic prophecy.

⟳ This study guide suggests that many of the prophecies in the book of Daniel have already been fulfilled, at least initially, by events that are now in the past, even though this doesn't rule out further fulfillments in the future. (Many interpreters, for example, also see Christ's sacrifice on the cross as a fulfillment of the statement that "the anointed one will be put to death.") How comfortable are you with this approach? How does it compare with other interpretations you've heard of the visions in the book of Daniel?

DANIEL'S VISION OF THE KINGS OF THE NORTH AND SOUTH

Book of Daniel > Visions > Fourth Vision

INTRODUCTION

Shortly after Cyrus allows the Jews to return home and rebuild the temple, Daniel has a final vision. It's so long, complex, and troubling that Daniel prays and fasts for three weeks to try to understand it. Finally a messenger from God, who's had to struggle the whole time to reach Daniel, arrives with the interpretation. He confirms the message of the earlier visions: At some time in the future, the temple, now being peacefully rebuilt, will once again be threatened with desolation and destruction. This fourth vision discloses that the threat will arise specifically in the course of a long and bitter rivalry between the "king of the South" and the "king of the North."

READING

Read through this last vision together as a group, having people take turns reading one paragraph at a time. (If you don't have copies of *The Books of The Bible* and you've been using the traditional chapter divisions as a guide to the sections in Daniel, note that this last section includes chapters 10, 11, and 12.)

DISCUSSION

1 The "man dressed in linen" explains to Daniel that he was sent immediately to interpret the vision, but he was delayed in battle with the "prince of the Persian kingdom" and was only able to continue his mission when Michael, "one of the chief princes," came to help him. This explanation gives us an intriguing glimpse into the unseen world of spiritual conflict that lies behind the outworking of God's purposes in the world. (In this case, God's purpose is to warn his people about the need to remain strong and faithful in the face of future danger.)

➲ Not to spook anybody, but have you ever felt that dark forces were at work to thwart the purposes God wanted to carry out through you or through a community of believers you were part of? What made you suspect there was more going on than met the eye? What particular means did these dark forces use to cause trouble? What counter-measures, if any, were you able to employ successfully? Did anyone pray and fast, the way Daniel does here?

2 This vision, like the previous three, has its initial fulfillment in events that have already taken place in the past. The "king of the South" and the "king of the North" are two dynasties that arose from the former empire of Alexander the Great. We've already been introduced to one of these dynasties: The "king of the North" represents the rulers of the Seleucid empire (founded by Alexander's general Seleucus), based in the former Babylonian territories. The "king of the South" is the Ptolemaic dynasty (founded by General Ptolemy) in Egypt. The vision traces the invasions, counter-invasions, and unsuccessful attempts at marriage alliances that characterized the rivalry between these dynasties in the 150 years after Alexander died. (See the map on page 27, and note how these two empires collided right where the Jewish people lived, putting them in the line of fire throughout the long rivalry.)

➲ Based on what you've discovered in the sessions devoted to Daniel's visions, explain how each of the following parts of this fourth vision was initially fulfilled in history. (Suggested answers are provided at the end of this session.)

- "A mighty king will arise, who will rule with great power and do as he pleases. After he has arisen, his empire will be broken up and parceled out toward the four winds of heaven."
- "The king of the South will become strong, but one of [the mighty king's] commanders will become even stronger than he and will rule his own kingdom with great power."
- "He will be succeeded by a contemptible person who has not been given the honor of royalty. He will . . . seize it through intrigue."
- "His armed forces will rise up to desecrate the temple fortress and will abolish the daily sacrifice. Then they will set up the abomination that causes desolation."

3 At some point, however, this vision shifts to the more distant future. It becomes harder and harder to correlate its details with known historical events, and the vision begins to describe things that clearly have not happened yet, such as the general resurrection of the dead ("multitudes who sleep in the dust of the earth will awake: some to everlasting life, others to shame and everlasting contempt").

A similar shift in focus, from the more immediate future to the more distant future, occurs in other biblical visions and prophecies, as a definitive crisis in the life of God's people evokes the ultimate crisis at the end of the age. (Jeremiah foretold the destruction of Babylon, for example, and in Revelation, John picks up Jeremiah's Babylon as an image of the destruction of Rome. The image of Babylon may indeed apply to future events from our standpoint.) So there is clearly a further, future fulfillment of Daniel's visions to be anticipated.

But Daniel himself was told he wouldn't understand everything he'd seen: "the words are closed up and sealed until the time of the end." So we shouldn't expect detailed insight into end-times events ourselves, either. Instead, we can follow the same counsel Daniel was given: "go your way till the end." We can keep following and serving God faithfully, and if we don't live to see this ultimate fulfillment, we will "rest" in death, and then at the "end of the days" rise from the dead to receive our "allotted inheritance."

◐ Think about how you felt about facing the future before you began this study of Daniel. Do you feel differently now? If so, what has changed, and why?

◐ What spiritual conflicts, "desolations," and challenges to compromise do followers of Jesus face in today's world? How does the example set by Daniel and his friends so long ago give us encouragement and inspiration for our own lives?

NOTE

Suggested answers for the question in section 2:

a. Alexander the Great conquers a vast empire but dies suddenly, and his empire is divided up among four of his generals.

b. Ptolemy secures an empire for himself in Egypt, while Seleucus bases an empire of his own in Babylon.

c. Antiochus IV Epiphanes becomes Seleucid emperor when three rightful successors are deposed or murdered. (This is symbolized in Daniel's first vision by three uprooted horns.)

d. Antiochus IV Epiphanes desecrates the temple and suppresses Jewish worship.

REVELATION

EXPERIENCING THE BOOK OF REVELATION AS A WHOLE

Book of Revelation (Overview)

INTRODUCTION

In this session your group will begin its study of Revelation by reading the whole book aloud together. As you hear the book read, you can see how it unfolds by following the outline on page 71. The map on page 72 shows the location of the seven churches the book is addressed to.

If have a copy of *The Books of The Bible*, begin by reading the introduction to Revelation on pages 1789–90. If you don't, the material on "Why Read and Study Daniel and Revelation?" at the beginning of this study guide, and the material in the rest of this introduction, will give you a basic sense of what the book is about.

As you listen to Revelation, you'll recognize that it has four main parts. The man named John who wrote the book says four different times that he was "in the Spirit," meaning that he was receiving a revelation from God. As he says this, he names four different locations where he saw himself in his vision: on the island of Patmos (his physical location), in heaven, in a wilderness, and on a mountain. These four locations correspond with different themes and emphases in the vision, as we'll see in later sessions. For now, as you listen, notice where these four parts begin. (Note, as the outline shows, that the "wilderness" part of the vision interrupts the "heaven" part, which then resumes for a little while after the "wilderness" part ends.)

The book of Revelation was written to warn about the same kind of impending crisis that the visions in the book of Daniel described. Daniel and his friends had been able to serve God faithfully in a foreign court, but Daniel was then warned in visions that a future emperor, Antiochus IV Epiphanes, would exalt himself as a god and violently suppress the worship of the true God. In the same way, followers of Jesus had been able to live peacefully and productively within the Roman Empire and count on its government to protect them from harm (with one notable exception that we'll learn more about as we study Revelation). But one of Jesus' followers was then warned, in the vision that inspired the book of Revelation, that a Roman emperor would be worshipped as a god and that anyone who didn't join in this worship would be persecuted.

Daniel's visions were for "the distant future," but the vision in the book of Revelation showed "what must soon take place." Its predictions began to be fulfilled within a few years after it was written. As the cities in the western part of the "province of Asia" (meaning Asia Minor or present-day Turkey) competed for the favor and patronage of the emperor Domitian (AD 81–96), they began to give him divine titles and honors. Followers of Jesus couldn't join in this emperor worship, and this put them on a collision course with the forces around them.

READING

Have the members of your group take turns reading through the book of Revelation out loud. It's on pages 1791–1812 in *The Books of The Bible*. If you're using another edition, you can find Revelation in its table of contents. (It's almost always the last book in the Bible.)

It should take only about an hour to read through the book. Change readers every time you come to one of the breaks marked by white space in *The Books of The Bible*. If you're using a different edition, change readers when you feel you've come to a natural break, for example, at the end of the sections marked on the outline on page 71 (such as "John's Vision of Jesus"). The traditional chapter divisions often don't correspond well with the sections in the book of Revelation, so don't rely on them as a guide, as you could for Daniel.

When it's your turn to read, think of yourself as telling the story to the rest of the group. If you prefer not to read aloud, just let the next person take their turn.

As your group reads through the book, listen for the "big picture" and notice how major themes are being developed.

DISCUSSION

⮑ Had you ever heard or read the book of Revelation before? If not, what did you think of it this first time through? If you had read the book before, but never heard it out loud, what was different about this experience?

⮑ What would you say are the major themes or "big ideas" that the book of Revelation develops? What things struck you most as you listened? What were your overall impressions?

⮑ What similarities did you notice between the books of Daniel and Revelation? What were some of the most important differences?

NOTE

The book of Revelation is interpreted in four major ways. The *futurist* approach understands it to be a description of the events of the "end times," at the end of human history. (Works like the novels and movies in the *Left Behind* series follow this approach.) The *historicist* view sees the book as a prediction of the whole course of history, from Jesus and the apostles down through the present to the end of the age. The *idealist* interpretation is that Revelation depicts the struggles and triumphs that followers of Jesus will experience everywhere, but it doesn't have any particular place or time in view. The *preterist* approach is to try to understand the book by reference to the time and place it was written in—western Asia Minor towards the close of the first century.

This study guide will consistently pursue a preterist interpretation. If this is new for you, and you're used to hearing the book treated differently, just try to keep an open mind and look for the potential benefits of this approach as you and your group do the following sessions together.

OUTLINE OF THE BOOK OF REVELATION

(Numbers correspond to sessions in this study guide)

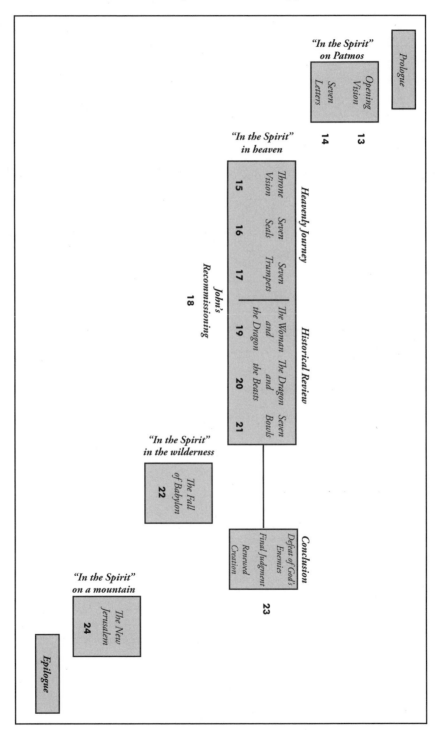

"In the Spirit" on Patmos

Prologue

Opening Vision — 13
Seven Letters — 14

"In the Spirit" in heaven

Heavenly Journey

Throne Vision — 15
Seven Seals — 16
Seven Trumpets — 17

John's Recommissioning — 18

Historical Review

The Woman and the Dragon — 19
The Dragon and the Beasts — 20
Seven Bowls — 21

"In the Spirit" in the wilderness

The Fall of Babylon — 22

Conclusion

Defeat of God's Enemies
Final Judgment
Renewed Creation — 23

"In the Spirit" on a mountain

The New Jerusalem — 24

Epilogue

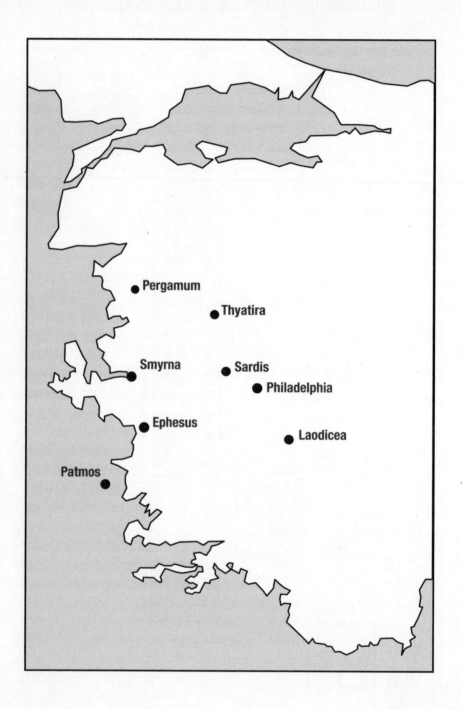

Pergamum

Thyatira

Smyrna

Sardis

Philadelphia

Ephesus

Laodicea

Patmos

"IN THE SPIRIT"
ON THE ISLAND OF PATMOS

JOHN'S VISION OF JESUS IN HIS GLORY

Book of Revelation > Prologue
Book of Revelation > "In the Spirit" on Patmos >
Opening Vision

INTRODUCTION

The person who received the vision recorded in the book of Revelation was named John. He was probably not the apostle John, who wrote one of the gospels (accounts of Jesus' life) and three of the letters in the New Testament. For one thing, that apostle never wrote in his own name, as Revelation's author does. Instead, he called himself "the disciple whom Jesus loved" or "the elder." For another thing, the language, themes, and perspectives of the apostle's writings are very different from those in Revelation. So the "John" who received this vision was most likely a different person, a traveling prophet who taught in several of the churches in the "province of Asia." In a foreshadowing of the persecution to come, John had been imprisoned on the nearby island of Patmos (see the map on page 72) because of "the word of God and the testimony of Jesus."

To warn others about the impending danger, John wrote a description of his vision and sent it out as a circular letter (that is, one letter that all of his churches could pass around and make copies of). That's why, after a title that explains the book's purpose, Revelation begins just as other letters did in the Roman world, with the sender's name, the recipient's name, a good wish, and words of praise to God. This letter-type opening serves as a prologue or introduction. But right after it, the book follows the general pattern of an *apocalypse*, the kind of writing that was introduced in session 8. You'll recall that in these works, a messenger from God "lifts the veil" and reveals the secrets of the future and of the heavenly realm. The person who's given this revelation describes how they received it, speaking in the first person (saying "I," "my," etc.).

In the book of Revelation, the messenger is Jesus Christ himself, raised from the dead and exalted in heaven after giving his life as the Savior of the world. He appears to John in the full glory of his heavenly exaltation. John uses the language and imagery of earlier Scriptures, particularly Daniel, to describe what he sees. He does this, for one thing, so that his readers can understand the significance of his vision in light of the written spiritual heritage of God's people. But drawing on the treasury of Scriptural phrases and images may also have been the only way John could put these extraordinary sights into words.

READING

Have one person read the title of the book of Revelation, which explains its purpose.

Have someone else read the letter-style opening. (It begins, "John, to the seven churches . . .")

Then have someone read John's description of his vision of Jesus (beginning, "I, John, your brother . . ." and ending ". . . the seven lampstands are the seven churches").

DISCUSSION

1 The book of Revelation gives us an important key to its own interpretation right in John's opening vision of Jesus. A couple of details are explained to illustrate that the whole book is meant to be understood *symbolically*. That is, it presents pictures that stand for something else, like the images in a dream. (The visions in Daniel worked the same way: animals, for example, symbolized kingdoms or kings.) We're told that "the seven lampstands are the seven churches." According to the book of Exodus, God commanded the Israelites to make a special golden lampstand for their place of worship. So this image provides a natural symbol for a worshipping community. The other symbol that's explained, to show how the book works, is, "The seven stars are the angels of the seven churches." Stars, as celestial objects, make a good symbol for heavenly beings. (These may be actual angels, something like "guardian angels" for each church, or they may represent the churches' leaders.)

These examples show us that this vision of Jesus isn't intended to describe what he actually looks like. Rather, it's symbolic. As we'll see when we consider its individual details, it's actually a depiction of his power and glory, to assure believers, faced with the impending crisis, that no enemy will ever defeat him or destroy the community of his followers.

⮑ The book of Daniel is one of John's main sources for words and images to express what he sees in Revelation. We can draw on our earlier studies to understand the symbolic meaning of the way he describes Jesus here. For example, based on what we saw in session 8, section 3, what's implied when John says that Jesus was "like a son of man"?

⮑ John also says of Jesus, "the hair on his head was white like wool." This is exactly how Daniel described the Ancient of Days. Recall what the phrase "ancient of days" means. What is John saying about Jesus? Why is white hair a good symbol for this? (Does this help you get a feel for how the symbolism of the book works?)

2 There are five similarities between the way Daniel described the "man dressed in linen" in his fourth vision and the way John describes Jesus here. In both cases the figure is described with:

- a golden sash/belt
- eyes like blazing fire/flaming torches
- feet/legs like burnished bronze
- a loud voice like a trumpet/multitude
- a bright face like the sun/lightning

Most interpreters agree that burning eyes symbolize that Jesus can see into everything, and thus knows everything. The loud voice symbolizes great power. The bright face, compared with a bright light in the sky, is symbolic of heavenly glory. Bronze feet suggest a formidable opponent (like the bronze claws of the fourth beast in Daniel's first vision). The golden sash represents wealth or authority.

⮑ Do you think of Jesus as being alive today and having the kind of attributes symbolized in this vision? Which attributes (discussed in this section and section 1) are the easiest for you to believe he has? Which are the most difficult? Why?

3 Besides the symbols that describe him, Jesus is given many titles in this opening section of the book. So is God the Father. These titles reveal more about their character and attributes.

⮑ As a group, go through the prologue and first vision in Revelation and find as many titles of Jesus or God as you can. Have someone in your group make a list. If it's not clear what a title means, discuss it together. (There's a suggested list of titles and their meanings at the end of this session.)

⮑ Which of the titles or attributes of Jesus is most encouraging or meaningful to you in your life right now? Why?

NOTE

Suggested answers for section 3, question 2:

God the Father is called:

- the one "who is, and who was, and who is to come" (describing his eternal existence)
- "the Alpha and the Omega" (these were the first and last letters of the Greek alphabet—it's like saying "the A and the Z," the beginning and the end of everything)

- "the Almighty" (having all power)

Jesus is called:

- "the faithful witness" (someone who stayed faithful to God and spoke about him)
- "the firstborn from the dead" (the first person to rise from the dead)
- "the ruler of the kings of the earth" (someone with supreme authority)
- "the First and the Last" (the beginning and end of everything)
- "the Living One" (someone who is truly alive and gives life to others)

THE LETTERS TO THE SEVEN CHURCHES

**Book of Revelation > "In the Spirit" on Patmos >
Seven Letters**

INTRODUCTION

The entire vision in the book of Revelation is addressed to each of the seven churches where the prophet John taught. But each church also gets an individual word of encouragement and admonition from the exalted Jesus, in the form of a letter.

Followers of Jesus living in western Asia Minor during the reign of Domitian are already beginning to experience persecution and temptations to compromise. These will intensify as the cult of emperor worship closes in on them. Jesus helps prepare them for the coming trials by speaking, through John, to the way they've been succeeding or failing as they face these initial tests.

One of their main challenges is coming from people who claim to be followers of Jesus, but who are teaching that it's all right to participate in the worship of Greek and Roman gods by going to their temples, eating food offered to them, and patronizing temple prostitutes. These false teachers are called "Nicolaitans," and they're compared with figures from the First Testament (Old Testament) such as Balaam and Jezebel, who similarly led God's people to compromise. Another challenge is coming from people in these cities, particularly in the Jewish synagogues, who are threatening Jesus' followers with imprisonment or even death because of their faith. One person, Antipas in Pergamum, has already given his life, and more persecution is coming.

These letters "lift the veil" and reveal the spiritual forces at work behind the temptations and persecution, and the true spiritual condition of the churches.

READING

Have seven people in your group take turns reading these letters out loud.

DISCUSSION

1 All of these letters follow the same pattern. At the *start* of each letter, after the "angel" of the church is addressed, Jesus describes himself by an image or title taken (in almost every case) from the book's opening. These images and titles are intentionally selected to portray Jesus as the one who's able to help each specific church meet the challenges it's facing:

Ephesus: The seven stars and lampstands are symbols of the churches and their leaders. Jesus has these, showing he's the head of the church, with the authority to "remove your lampstand." This should make the church eager to recapture its first love and avoid this fate.

Smyrna: A church threatened with deadly persecution will be encouraged by the way Jesus "died and came to life again."

Pergamum: The double-edged sword symbolizes the word of God. (What comes out of Jesus' mouth is the word of God.) This true word will clean up a church infested with false teachers.

Thyatira: The all-seeing eyes of Jesus expose the "deep secrets" of false teachers.

Sardis: The "seven spirits" are the seven-fold Spirit or Holy Spirit of God, who will give life to this church that is "about to die."

Philadelphia: The "key of David" refers to Jesus' Messianic authority; it seems to be the same as "the keys of death and Hades" in the opening vision.

Jesus will open a door "that no one can shut" so that this beleaguered church can continue its witness.

Laodicea: Only the phrase "faithful . . . witness" comes directly from the book's opening vision. (But when Jesus is called "the ruler of God's creation," this is similar to him being called "the ruler of the kings of the earth" in the opening vision.) This church is not bearing true or faithful witness to its own spiritual condition, which Jesus can help them recognize.

➲ If you're a regular part of the life and worship of a community of Jesus' followers, try to decide what attribute of Jesus, symbolized in these letters and the opening vision of the book, is most needed to help your church meet its greatest challenge. (Group members who attend the same church can form a team and discuss this.) People who don't attend any one church regularly can work together to decide what attribute is most needed to help the whole community of Jesus' followers in their town, district, or city. Get back together as a group and discuss your conclusions. Let anyone who's comfortable doing so pray to Jesus, addressing him by these attributes, to ask him to help their church.

2 At the *end* of each letter, "whoever has ears" is urged to "hear what the Spirit says to the churches," and a promise is made to "those who are victorious." Most of these promises use images that will be introduced and developed later in the book. For example, the last letter ends, "to those who are victorious, I will give the right to sit with me on my throne, just as I was victorious and sat down with my Father on his throne." In the very next scene, we'll see Jesus received at the throne of God.

➲ Were you ever promised a reward for reaching a goal? If so, tell the group what the promised reward was, and whether you reached your goal and received it.

➲ Which of the rewards described in these letters would you most like to receive? Why?

◗ What would you like God to do for you if you're successful in meeting the greatest spiritual challenge you're facing right now? Give people a few minutes to think about this and to talk to God about it in silent prayer.

3 In the *main body* of each letter, the church is commended and corrected, and given a challenge. The commendation usually begins, "I know . . ." and the correction usually begins, "I have this against you . . ." (Some churches aren't corrected, while others aren't commended.) For example, the church in Ephesus is commended, among other things, for "your deeds, your hard work and your perseverance"; it's corrected for forsaking "the love you had at first"; and it's challenged to "repent and do the things you did at first."

◗ Following the same pattern as these letters, and using their commendations, corrections, and challenges as examples, have each individual in the group privately write a letter from Jesus to a modern-day community of his followers. Write from the heart, but use discretion as you decide who to show your letter to. Pray about the possibility of humbly and respectfully sharing your letter with one or more of the leaders of the church it's addressed to.

"IN THE SPIRIT"
IN HEAVEN

THE LAMB BEFORE THE HEAVENLY THRONE

**Book of Revelation > "In the Spirit" in Heaven >
Heavenly Journey > Throne Vision**

INTRODUCTION

After the letters to the seven churches, the second major section of the book of Revelation begins. The letters describe present conditions, while what John sees in this next section depicts "what must take place after this," as the emperor cult emerges and threatens the community of Jesus' followers.

John hears the same voice (the voice of Jesus) that first called him to write down what he saw. "In the Spirit" once again, he takes a journey up to God's throne room. There, in an extended series of visions, he first views the impending spiritual conflict from the perspective of heaven; later, he sees symbolically how it will play out on earth.

In the opening vision of his heavenly journey, John is introduced to the life of heaven. He witnesses ever-widening circles of creatures continually worshipping God as the eternally-existing creator, and worshipping Jesus as the redeemer of the world.

READING

In this vision, John's descriptions of what he sees in heaven lead up to five songs of praise. (In most Bibles, these songs are printed as poetry within the narrative, so they're easy to recognize.) Have five members of your group serve as narrators and read the descriptions that lead up to the songs. When you get to them, have everyone read the songs aloud together. They are:

- The song of the four living creatures ("Holy, holy, holy . . .")
- The song of the twenty-four elders ("You are worthy, our Lord and God . . .")
- The song of the living creatures and the elders ("You are worthy to take the scroll . . .")
- The song of the angels ("Worthy is the Lamb, who was slain . . .")
- The song of every creature ("To him who sits on the throne . . .")

(There's one more line for the fifth narrator to read after the last song.)

DISCUSSION

1 Does John's vision show us what it's really like in heaven? Who are these creatures with animal faces and wings and eyes all over? Who are the "twenty-four elders" with robes and crowns and thrones? Some of the details in this vision may reflect the actual sights and sounds of heaven; it's impossible to say how many. To describe what he sees, John continues to borrow from the language and imagery of earlier Scriptures. (For example, like the Ancient of Days in Daniel, God is surrounded here by angels numbering "thousands upon thousands, and ten thousand times ten thousand.")

As we've noted, allusions like this communicate the significance of each element in John's vision against the background of the spiritual heritage of God's people. It also helps John put these extraordinary sights into words. We can at least interpret the parts of the vision that are expressed this way. And we can let the vision as a whole transport us into the never-ending worship that surrounds God's throne in heaven.

Many of the details of this vision are described in language that's shared with the opening of the book of Ezekiel: the four living creatures with multiple wings and faces like a lion, an ox, an eagle, and a human being; eyes all around; flashes of lightning; the throne; the rainbow; and the scroll. John wants his readers to appreciate the continuity between the prophet Ezekiel's vision of heaven and the word that God is bringing in his own day.

The four living creatures represent creation as it is praising God. Their faces depict leading representatives of various created spheres: domesticated animals (the ox), wild animals (the lion), creatures of the air (the eagle), and people, who have dominion over all of creation. The twenty-four elders are representatives of the community of God's followers, both before and after the coming of Jesus. Their number reflects the ancestors of the twelve tribes of Israel plus the twelve apostles. (This same symbolism appears at the end of the book, in the description of the New Jerusalem.) These elders have received what is promised in the letters to "those who are victorious": white robes, crowns, and thrones.

As the vision culminates, everything created and everyone redeemed joins with countless angels to praise and worship God, showing that this is what life in heaven centers around.

⊃ What's the greatest worship experience you've ever been part of? What made it so great? (Share two or three experiences if you can't decide on just one.)

2 In addition to visual symbols drawn from earlier Scriptures, the book of Revelation also uses numerical symbols. Certain numbers in the book are like "logos" that point to key characters and themes. This vision illustrates what several of these numbers stand for.

Three represents God, who's often described in three-part phrases ("who was, and is, and is to come") and ascribed triple attributes ("holy, holy, holy"; "glory and honor and power.")

Four is the number of creation. Creation is represented in this vision by four living creatures, and it's also described as having four parts: heaven, earth, under-earth, and sea. The song of every creature ascribes four attributes to the Lamb: praise, honor, glory, and power. We'll see other uses of the number four to symbolize creation as the book continues (for example, in the next vision, "four angels standing at the four corners of the earth, holding back the four winds").

The number seven (4+3) represents perfection and completeness. The Lamb has seven horns and seven eyes; these symbolize his absolute power and knowledge. The scroll has seven seals because it contains the definitive judgments of God. Earlier we saw seven churches symbolized by seven lampstands and seven stars. While these are actual churches, they're also representative of the church as a whole; what's written to them is also addressed to the wider community of Jesus' followers. We've heard several times about the "seven spirits of God," depicted here as seven lamps. As the TNIV translation note explains, this is the "sevenfold Spirit"—the perfect (divine) Holy Spirit. The angels, in their song, ascribe seven attributes to the Lamb, acknowledging his divine perfections.

Twelve (4x3) represents the community of God's followers. It appears in the book by itself and in various combinations, such as the 12+12 elders in this vision.

⮑ Working alone or on a team with others from your group, design a logo, slogan, or icon that expresses how you understand and relate to one or more of the following: God, creation, perfection, community. Draw on the numerical symbolism of Revelation if you wish. Share your designs with the rest of the group.

3 The centerpiece of this vision is the appearance of the "Lion of the tribe of Judah," who turns out to be, paradoxically, "a Lamb, looking as if it had been slain." This refers to the way Jesus gave his life on the cross as the "Lamb of God," and through his death brought salvation to everyone who believes in him. And so Jesus has "triumphed." This is the same Greek word used to describe "those who are victorious" in the seven letters. Victory in the struggle against the emperor cult will come not through violent resistance, but through suffering, sacrifice, and death, following in the steps of Jesus, who gave his life for the world.

⮑ In what ways do people today, in your own culture, suffer because they are followers of Jesus? Have you ever seen these sufferings turn into what you would call a "victory"? If so, how did this happen?

4 This vision of heavenly worship has inspired countless hymns and songs over the centuries. These include the closing chorus of Handel's *Messiah*, the hymn "Holy, Holy, Holy, Lord God Almighty," and more recent compositions such as "Worthy is the Lamb" ("Thank You For the Cross") by Darlene Zschech, "We Fall Down" by Chris Tomlin, and "Agnus Dei" by Michael W. Smith.

➲ What other songs or hymns do you know that allude to this vision? Which are your favorites, and why?

➲ Conclude your time together, if you wish, by watching an online video of Kari Jobe singing "Revelation Song," another recent composition inspired by this vision. (Go to www.youtube.com/watch?v=FObjd5wrgZ8, or search online if the video has moved.)

THE LAMB OPENS THE SEVEN SEALS

INTRODUCTION

John has seen Jesus Christ honored by heaven and all of creation as the "Lamb who was slain" for the salvation of the world. His death was God's definitive means of bringing people back into relationship with himself. As the redeemer, Jesus is given the authority to execute God's purposes, which are to extend either judgment or mercy to people based on how they respond to this initiative. These purposes are represented by a seven-sealed scroll, and Jesus now sets them in motion by opening its seals.

READING

Have six people take turns reading the descriptions of what happens as the Lamb opens each of the first six seals.

There's an interlude between the sixth and seventh seal. (It begins, "After this I saw four angels . . ."). Read this like a play, with people taking these parts:

Narrator	One of the elders
Angel from the east	John

In this play, have the whole group read the song of the great multitude ("Salvation belongs to our God . . .") and the song of the angels ("Amen! Praise and glory . . .").

Finally, have someone read what happens when the Lamb opens the seventh seal. (It's just one sentence.)

DISCUSSION

1 The seven seals are the first of three series of seven divine judgments in the book of Revelation. Later seven trumpets will sound, and then seven bowls will be poured out.

These series can't be understood both *literally* and *sequentially*, since the sun, moon, and stars vanish with the sixth seal, but they're nevertheless in the sky at the time of the fourth trumpet, and the sun is affected by the fifth bowl. So it seems best to understand these series *symbolically*, as descriptions of the *purposes* God is carrying out through his judgments.

The interlude between the sixth and seventh seals points to the purpose of this series. It "zooms in" on the fifth seal and explains in more detail about the people in white robes and the "full number" that will be gathered before God. The numerical symbolism of the book is out in force as the community of Jesus' followers is described in its fullness as 12 x 12 x 10 x 10 x 10. (Twelve, as we've seen, is the numerical "logo" of this community; ten, like seven, is a number that symbolizes totality and completeness.)

The people who are "sealed" here aren't literal Israelites. The combination of tribal names, and their order, is unlike any description of Israel earlier in the Scriptures. Rather, the "144,000 from all the tribes of Israel" is a symbol. It represents the full number of people who will become followers of Jesus. This interpretation is confirmed in the text: John *hears* the 144,000 announced, but what he then *sees* is "a great multitude that no one could count, from every nation, tribe, people and language" worshipping the Lamb.

God wants to bring this great multitude into relationship with himself. He's willing to delay the just consequences due to those who have violently oppressed others, including his own followers, so that the full number can be brought in. Therefore, the overall flow of the opening of the seven seals is judgment announced, but then delayed, for the sake of those who may still believe ("until we put a seal on the foreheads of the servants of our God").

⮑ What's the closest you've come in your life to being in "a great multitude that no one could count, from every nation, tribe, people and language," that has gathered in one place to serve and worship God?

⮑ God appears to you in a dream and offers you a choice. You can die and enter into eternal blessings immediately, or you can live many more years on earth, experiencing difficult trials and sufferings, and see several friends and loved ones come to Christ as a result. Which do you choose?

2 Judgments are announced in the first four seals, but their full ultimate effect (depicted by the sixth seal) is delayed: The earth and its inhabitants will be spared for a time so that God can call more people into relationship with himself. Nevertheless, these judgments have been let loose on the earth, and they may actually play a role in bringing people to God. The misfortunes that God permits may help people realize their need for him. The forces of conflict, strife, and economic disparity may also prevent humanity from uniting together to oppose God. So the judgments that are released help fulfill the purpose of the seals as a whole: to gather a great multitude before God's throne.

⮑ If misfortune, violence, and inequity can help people find God, are we working against God when we work against those forces? (There's a suggested answer to this question at the end of the session that you can interact with once you've all shared your own thoughts.)

3 When the fifth seal is opened, those who have given their lives for Jesus appear "under the altar," since they've given their lives as a sacrifice. They're told to "wait a little longer," not for the full number of those who will *believe*, but for the full number of those who will be *killed*. John is warning that soon anyone who chooses to follow Jesus will need to be prepared to give their life for him: Everyone in the "great multitude" is wearing a white robe, showing that they're all martyrs, or they're willing to be.

Here Revelation describes the coming period of deadly persecution as "the great tribulation," meaning a time of severe trial. Followers of Jesus in other times and places have also experienced their own "great tribulations," when many of them have been killed for their faith. Many interpreters believe that there will be a climactic conflict between good and evil at the end of this age of human history, and at that time, followers of Jesus all over the world will experience the same kind of "great tribulation."

➲ Why do you think God allows so many of his followers to be killed by those who oppose him? Does God see some positive value in their deaths?

➲ Would you want to be a follower of Jesus if you knew it could cost you your life? If your answer is yes, why would it be worth it to die for him?

NOTE

Suggested answer to the question in section 2: God doesn't want destructive things to happen at all; he'd much rather have people turn to him without them. But sometimes people (individually or corporately) resist God so stubbornly that he allows them to carry out their own plans and experience the destructive consequences, so that they can recognize a better way. This is what divine "judgments" often are in the Bible. So when followers of Jesus oppose violence and economic disparity and try to relieve suffering, they're actually working in harmony with God's purposes, because they're demonstrating the kind of world God really wants in the first place. And when they experience suffering themselves, they're being "followers" of Jesus in the truest sense, by going through just what he went through to help realize God's purposes for the world.

THE SEVEN ANGELS SOUND THEIR TRUMPETS

**Book of Revelation > "In the Spirit" in Heaven >
Heavenly Journey > The Seven Trumpets**

INTRODUCTION

John now sees a second series of divine judgments unfold: seven angels sound their trumpets. There are many similarities between this series and the previous one. In both cases there's an interlude between the sixth and seventh judgments. (We'll consider this interlude in our next session.) Both series begin with four judgments that are grouped together and described more briefly. The purpose of both sets of judgments is the same: to try to draw people away from destructive patterns of life and back into relationship with God. Unfortunately, not everyone responds positively: John marvels, after seeing the first six trumpets, how people "still did not repent of the work of their hands . . . their murders, their magic arts, their sexual immorality or their thefts."

READING

Have someone read the introduction to the trumpet judgments ("And I saw the seven angels who stand before God . . .).

Then have six people take turns reading the descriptions of what happens as the first six angels sound their trumpets. (The sixth reader ends, ". . . repent of their murders, their magic arts, their sexual immorality or their thefts.")

DISCUSSION

1 Once again it's not possible to take this series of judgments both *literally* and *sequentially*. "All the green grass," for example, is "burned up" by the first trumpet, but the locusts of the fifth trumpet are told "not to harm the grass of the earth." So this series, too, should be understood *symbolically*.

The first four seal judgments were associated with creation by their number (four) and by the way they were announced by the "living creatures." The first four trumpet judgments are similarly associated with creation by their number and by the way they affect different spheres within creation itself: the land, the sea, the fresh waters, and the sky. The plagues depicted here are described in the language of the earlier Scriptures. They're like several of the plagues God sent against Pharaoh when he refused to set the people of Israel free from slavery: hail mixed with fire, waters turning to blood and becoming undrinkable, the sky becoming dark. The overall message is that God may use natural forces as instruments of his judgment and correction.

➲ When natural disasters occur today, is God punishing the people who suffer from them? Say which of the following you agree with most:

   a. Every time a natural disaster occurs, God must be punishing somebody.
   b. Most natural disasters are "random," but God might send some of them as punishments.
   c. God doesn't want there to be natural disasters, but when there are, he uses them to shake up people's complacency and give them the opportunity to show compassion.
   d. (Some other explanation.)

➲ Can the suffering caused by disasters help bring about positive change? If so, how?

◯ If God works through natural disasters in any way to affect people, is it fair that creation itself has to suffer because of this?

2 At the fifth seal, the martyrs asked, "How long, Sovereign Lord . . . until you judge the inhabitants of the earth and avenge our blood?" The purpose of the trumpet judgments, besides trying to get people to repent of the wrong things they're doing, may be to start answering the martyrs' cry for justice by bringing some retribution against those who have killed God's servants. Each judgment under the first four trumpets affects "a third" of some part of creation. This phrase "a third" appears twelve times* as the first four trumpets are sounded. This is may indicate that these judgments are on behalf of the covenant community, symbolized in Revelation by the number twelve.

◯ If people continue to resist God, even to the point of violently attacking those who are working for good in the world, do you think a point comes where God's efforts shift from correction to retribution (payback), in the interests of justice? Explain your view.

3 Many different explanations have been offered of what happens when the fifth and sixth trumpets sound. It's a challenge for any explanation to account for all of the details in these descriptions. One possibility is that these two trumpets are depicting the same reality, first more symbolically and then more realistically. (A similar shift, from a more symbolic portrayal to a more literal portrayal, occurred with the 144,000 and the great multitude.)

To offer an interpretation in keeping with the preterist approach of this study guide, at the time the book of Revelation was written, this massive army crossing the Euphrates would have represented a devastating invasion of the Roman Empire by the fierce, long-haired Parthian hordes to the east. Since Rome eventually did fall to barbarians from the east, this is a fair depiction of the demise of the empire that systematically persecuted Jesus' followers. This interpretation is supported by the reference to "idols of gold, silver, bronze,

---

* The phrase appears 13 times in the TNIV, but the phrase "also a third of the night" is not a literal translation. The original Greek says simply, "and likewise the night."

stone and wood," an allusion to the story in Daniel of how Babylon fell to the invading Persians.

⮑ Where would you place your own society or civilization in a life cycle extending from birth and growth through expansion and flourishing to decline and collapse?

⮑ Is the fate of civilizations directly tied to the way they relate to God? Can they extend their lives by honoring God in particular ways? Will they meet an untimely end if they don't? What are the implications for us?

JOHN'S MISSION TO WARN
GOD'S PEOPLE IS RENEWED

INTRODUCTION

In the interlude between the sixth and seventh trumpets, John's mission to warn God's people of the coming persecution is renewed.

John has been commissioned to tell God's servants what must "soon take place." As we've seen in sessions 15 through 17, he's been taken up to heaven in a vision, where he's witnessed the worship of the angels and all creation centering on Jesus, the "Lamb who was slain" for the salvation of the world. He's seen Jesus begin to carry out God's purposes to gather a great multitude "from every nation, tribe, people and language" into a community to serve and worship him forever. Many people are still resisting and rejecting God, but their world is being shaken by plagues and disasters so that they'll turn away from the destructive things they're doing. For those who ultimately turn to God, the judgments of the seals and trumpets will be correction; for those who resist to the end, they will be justice and retribution. The message of the heavenly vision, for those who are suffering for their faith in Jesus, is that they should "wait a little longer" until God's purposes are carried out. They can be confident of the rewards God has promised to "those who are victorious," that is, those who stay faithful even to death.

But God has a further message to send to his people through John. (We'll consider this part of his vision in sessions 19, 20, 21, and 23.) He wants them to understand more about the specific threat they will be facing—a cult of emperor worship—so that they can recognize it when it arises and make no compromise with it. And so, in a continuation of the vision that began when he was called up into heaven, after the seventh trumpet sounds, John will be shown how events on earth will unfold in the near future.

But first, as we'll see here in session 18, John's mission to warn God's people, originally given to him in the opening vision of the book, is renewed: "you must prophesy again about many peoples, nations, languages and kings." (To follow how the book is developing at this point, it may be helpful to review the outline on page 71.)

READING

Read out loud, like a play, the accounts of John's mission being renewed and of the seventh trumpet being sounded. (Begin with, "Then I saw another mighty angel coming down from heaven." End with the description of God's temple being opened in heaven after the seventh trumpet sounds.) Have people find and read these parts:

Narrator

Voice from heaven

Angel (in addition to the two lines attributed directly to "the angel," this actor should also speak the two parts that begin, "You must prophesy again . . ." and "Go and measure the temple . . .")

Loud voices in heaven (several people can share this part)

Elders (everyone else can read this part together)

DISCUSSION

1 To show that his mission is genuinely from God, John draws extensively on the language and imagery of the earlier Scriptures. The angel who lifts his hand to heaven and swears "by him who lives for ever and ever," and who tells John to seal up what he hears, is much like the "man clothed in linen" at the end of Daniel's fourth vision. The little scroll that tastes like honey is like the one Ezekiel eats when he's first appointed as a prophet. Ezekiel also recounts, at the end of his book, how he saw the temple measured with a rod. Through the biblical images he uses here, as throughout the book of Revelation, John puts the full weight of the prophetic tradition, like the mass of a mile-long freight train, behind his warning against compromise.

➲ John's use of Scriptural language is a symbolic portrayal of the way he speaks for God genuinely and with authority. What actual marks in a person's life, words, and influence authenticate that they're truly speaking on God's behalf? (To use John as an example, for one thing, he's living consistently with his own message: He's already in exile because of "the testimony of Jesus.")

➲ When John says that the scroll was sweet in his mouth but bitter in his stomach, he's describing the joy and thrill of speaking God's words, and then the distress caused by people's hostile reactions to them. Have you ever had an experience like this?

2 The periods of 42 months and 1260 days are equivalent to three and a half years, the "time, times and half a time" of Daniel's first vision, when the "holy people" were "delivered into his hands," that is, those of Antiochus IV Epiphanes. John is warning, in evocative terms, that another time is coming when God's people will be put under severe pressure to abandon their faith. But even during this time, they can give a powerful testimony that will ultimately lead their opponents to give "glory to the God of heaven."

This testimony is represented here by the figures of the "two witnesses." They, too, are described in the language of the earlier Scriptures. In an allusion to the fifth vision in the book of Zechariah, they're described as "olive trees" and "lampstands," to show that their witness succeeds "not by might nor by power, but by [God's] Spirit." The witnesses are also described as like Moses, who turned the waters to blood, and like Elijah, who shut up the sky so that it would not rain. They may therefore represent "the Law and the

Prophets," that is, the word of God, accompanied by works of power, that Jesus' followers will proclaim even to those who are oppressing them.

⊃ Even if we don't strike other people with plagues, they may respond with hostility when we try to tell them about what God has done in our lives. Why do you think they do this? If you've ever found a way to overcome someone's initial hostility and share your story of faith in Jesus with them, tell the rest of the group how you did this.

3 The witnesses' most powerful testimony comes when they're raised from the dead. Their enemies deny them immediate burial—an outrage in this culture. But by doing this, these enemies are actually declaring God's purposes without realizing it: the witnesses aren't destined for the grave, but for resurrection. This part of their story illustrates what a powerful testimony Jesus' followers will give by being willing to die, knowing that God will raise them from the dead.

⊃ What do you expect to happen to you after you die?

THE WOMAN AND THE DRAGON

Book of Revelation > "In the Spirit" in Heaven > Historical Review > Woman and Dragon

INTRODUCTION

Many of the apocalypses known from the ancient world trace a pattern of historical developments that lead their readers up to a point of crisis. The book of Daniel, for example, describes a succession of four empires, and then a series of ten kings in the last empire, culminating in the crisis under Antiochus IV Epiphanes. The book of Revelation similarly traces how the crisis that it's warning about has emerged. But its historical review is more compressed. It begins only a couple of generations before the book was written, with the birth of Jesus. In vivid symbolism drawn from earlier Scriptures, Revelation traces how he came into the world and how his reign came under assault from the forces that have deceived and oppressed people throughout the ages. We'll look at the first part of this historical review in this session and then finish it in the next one.

READING

Have one person who has good dramatic expression read John's vision of the woman and the dragon (ending with the description of the dragon going off to make war against the rest of her offspring). Have others in the group silently act out the events during the reading, playing these parts:

> The woman
> The dragon
> The woman's son
> Michael and his angels
> The dragon's angels
> Loud voice in heaven
> The earth

(The actors should read through the passage together first to plan their performance.)

DISCUSSION

1 John first describes how Jesus came from the nation of Israel as the Messiah, the ruler and deliverer sent by God. The imagery of the sun, moon, and twelve stars identifies the woman in this vision as a symbol of Israel. This imagery is drawn from a dream that Joseph, one of the ancestors of the Israelite tribes, had. (It's recorded in the book of Genesis.)

The woman's son is identified as the Messiah by the phrase, he "will rule all the nations with an iron scepter," a quotation from Psalm 2 (translated there in the TNIV "you will break them with a rod of iron").

We're told within the vision itself that the dragon represents the devil. The seven crowned heads (a number of completeness) symbolize the devil's authority over every part of the world that's in resistance to God. The ten horns (another number of completeness), an image drawn from Daniel's first vision, depict the dragon's great power.

The dragon attempts to devour the woman's son: the gospels record how Jesus' life was in danger from the moment he was born, and how his enemies ultimately killed him. But God raised him from the dead and he ascended to heaven (he was "snatched up to God and to his throne"). From there, ever since, he's been leading a growing insurgency against the world's entrenched forces of injustice and oppression.

⮑ What's it like to think of Jesus as a character in a story that also has a seven-headed red dragon and a woman in celestial clothes? Does this make his life and ministry seem more like fantasy than reality? Or does it make them seem more real, by associating them with the universal elements of the heroic, monsters-and-maidens stories that people in all places and times enjoy?

2 The centerpiece of this vision is a depiction of how Jesus' sacrifice on the cross ("the blood of the Lamb") has destroyed the power of the devil. This is illustrated by a war in heaven between the "the dragon and his angels" (who are symbolized earlier in the vision by the stars swept out of the sky) and "Michael and his angels." Michael is a figure from the book of Daniel, a "prince" or "army commander" who fights on behalf of God's people. But behind this dramatic military symbolism lies the reality that the devil's power is actually very subtle and insidious: it's the power of *accusation*. To emphasize this, John describes the dragon by the Greek word *diabolos*, translated here as "devil" but literally meaning "accuser," and by the Hebrew word *satan*, which also means "accuser." Because of Christ's sacrifice, there are no longer any grounds for those who trust in Jesus to be accused before God. The devil is effectively "tossed out of court."

⮑ Work together as a group to explain how Jesus' death on the cross removes all grounds of accusation against those who trust in him.

⮑ While those who trust in Jesus can't be accused before God, they may still hear accusing voices in their own heads: "what you did was so bad, you can never be forgiven"; "you'll never make anything out of your life"; "you'll never change"; etc. How can the reality of what Jesus has done for us become such a powerful truth in our minds and hearts that it silences these voices?

3 Many interpreters believe that the story of the woman's escape from the dragon recapitulates how Jewish followers of Jesus escaped from Jerusalem during the Jewish-Roman war of AD 66–70. John, who wrote the book of Revelation, appears to have been among those who escaped. In the spring of AD 68, they fled across the Jordan River. It was swollen with spring floods, but it unexpectedly subsided enough to permit them to cross. This was like the Israelites crossing the Red Sea to escape from Egypt, when, as Moses said, God carried them "on eagles' wings." On the other side of the Jordan, these Jewish followers of Jesus reached the city of Pella, where Gentile Christians from Galilee provided for them throughout the period of danger.

So the woman's son escapes from the dragon, and then the woman does herself. Furious, the dragon goes after "the rest of her offspring"—meaning Gentile believers in Jesus living throughout the empire. John, who migrated to Asia Minor after fleeing from Jerusalem, sees the devil's fury at failing to destroy Jesus and his Jewish followers as the spiritual background to the persecution that will soon strike the Gentile churches where he teaches.

⮱ Re-read the final portion of this story (the part after the voice in heaven speaks) and match its symbols with the historical details of the escape from Jerusalem in AD 68.

⮱ Where in our world today do we see resistance to the coming reign of Jesus that's so evil it must be an expression of the "dragon's" furious opposition?

THE DRAGON AND THE BEASTS

Book of Revelation > "In the Spirit" in Heaven > Historical Review > Dragon and Beasts

INTRODUCTION

As Revelation continues to trace the historical developments that have led up to the present crisis, it now focuses on the cult of emperor worship that has emerged to threaten the very existence of the community of Jesus' followers.

READING

Have several people each read a paragraph of John's vision of the dragon and the beasts, ending with the description of the "number of the beast," 666.

DISCUSSION

1 Daniel, in his first vision, saw four beasts coming up out of the sea. The first was like a lion, the next like a bear, and the third like a leopard. The fourth was "terrifying and frightening and very powerful" and had ten horns. The beast that the dragon brings out of the sea here in Revelation is all of these rolled into one. Just as the "little horn" that came from the fourth beast "was waging war against the holy people and defeating them," so the beast that the dragon brings out of the sea "was given power to make war against God's people and to conquer them."

Since Daniel's beasts represented empires, this beast likely represents the empire John is living in: Rome. But it's an empire gone bad. It has become so unjust and oppressive that it has lost the God-given legitimacy behind human governments. It now controls its people through the power of evil.

Under most conditions, followers of Jesus should be loyal citizens of their countries and support their governments, as Daniel and his friends did when they served in the Babylonian and Persian courts. But under some conditions, like the ones Daniel foresaw and the ones described here, Jesus' followers need to refuse any cooperation with a government whose rulers turn demonic, defy God, and trample their own people.

➲ What examples can you give of evil rulers taking over countries so that their governments lose legitimacy and people of conscience need to resist rather than cooperate? How can we tell when a government has reached this point, or is approaching it? Is this something that will inevitably happen in various places and times, simply because of the evil in the world? Or can it somehow be prevented?

➲ What can people outside these countries do to support those who are working for freedom and justice from within, as they suffer with "patient endurance and faithfulness"?

2 A few years into his reign (AD 81–96), the emperor Domitian assumed the titles *dominus et deus*, "Lord and God." Imperial coins began to portray him with divine symbols. On one coin, for example, he's holding a thunderbolt, like the god Zeus. As the wealthy cities of western Asia Minor competed for Domitian's favor and patronage, they tried to outdo one another in paying him divine honors. Anyone who wouldn't join in was persecuted.

The second beast in this vision likely symbolizes this cult of emperor worship, since it leads the people to idolize the first beast (Rome, embodied in its emperor). This emperor worship may have been accompanied by "signs" such as those described in this passage. The "mark of the beast" that people need in order to buy and sell may represent Domitian's blasphemous coins, which would be held in the right hand for transactions. Coins were sometimes also worn in a band on the forehead, and this may explain some of the background to the symbol of people having the "mark of the beast" on their foreheads. However, having a name written there will be a powerful symbol of identity in several places later in Revelation, so this background is only a starting point for understanding the symbol—it shouldn't limit its meaning.

⊃ Would you still use your country's currency if it proclaimed your head of state as "Lord and God"? If you wouldn't, how do you think this would affect your life?

⊃ In most schools in the United States, at the beginning of each day students are required to stand and say, "I pledge allegiance to the flag of the United States of America, and to the republic for which it stands . . ." Some states have passed laws (these have been challenged in the courts) allowing schools to punish students who refuse to say the pledge. Are you in favor of such laws? Why or why not? In your explanation, compare this situation (or a similar one from your own culture) with the one here in Revelation.

3 Nero, Roman emperor from AD 54–68, was remembered as a tyrant and a murderer. He executed many of his opponents and was widely believed to have killed his mother and stepbrother to consolidate his power. He was also suspected of causing a great fire in Rome to clear the ground so he could build himself a huge palace. But Nero blamed the Christians in the city for the fire, and they were severely persecuted. When his generals finally revolted against him, to avoid execution Nero committed suicide by stabbing himself in the throat. But rumors circulated that Nero was still alive or would come back to life, and that he would reclaim his throne and resume his despotic reign.

John's vision of the "beast" can be understood against this background. The "beast" appears to be a depiction of the current emperor as if he were Nero come back to life. That is, Domitian will become a tyrant like Nero and persecute the followers of Jesus the way he did. And so he's described as "the beast who was wounded by the sword and yet lived."

The "number of the beast," 666, also points to Nero come back to life. In many ancient languages, letters were used to represent numbers. (One example of this is the "Roman numerals" we know today: Super Bowl XLIV means Super Bowl 44.) Words and names in these languages had a total value, the sum of their letters. Apocalypses would sometimes play on the symbolic significance of these totals. 666 means falling short of divinity or perfection, symbolized by the number 7. But whose name adds up to this total, revealing the hollowness of his pretensions to divinity? John writes that "this calls for wisdom," meaning that the puzzle has a trick to it. Even though he's writing his book in Greek, the numerical values will be those of Hebrew letters. The consonants of "Nero Caesar" in Hebrew add up to 666. Domitian thinks he's "lord and God," but he's really just another evil emperor. Tagging Domitian with the name of Nero is like drawing a Hitler mustache on a leader's picture today.

⮕ Do you agree or disagree with the following statement? Explain why.

"The meaning of the 'number of the beast,' 666, has a unique solution based on the conventions of apocalypses and the facts of history. Its main purpose is to delegitimize Domitian's claims to divinity and to strengthen followers of Jesus who are being pressured by the emperor cult. Evil rulers in other places and times may also revive the tyrannical spirit of Nero, and they'll have to be resisted with suffering and endurance. But the number 666 isn't a coded biblical prediction of some invisible, demonic means of social control in the end times."

⮕ An Asian friend of yours gives you a piece of artwork with a large swastika in the center. It's an ancient symbol of prosperity and good fortune in their culture. But you live in a Western country where the swastika is associated with Hitler and the Nazis. Do you display the artwork in your home? Explain.

NOTE

In another example of finding symbolic significance in the total value of a name, an early Christian apocalyptic writer says that the "son of the great God" is the one whose name adds up to 888. This is the value of the letters of "Jesus" in Greek (*Iesous*). (8 is the number of resurrection, since Jesus was raised on the first day of a new week, the day after the 7th day.)

ANGELS POUR OUT SEVEN BOWLS

Book of Revelation > "In the Spirit" in Heaven > Historical Review > The Seven Bowls

INTRODUCTION

God has asked his people for "patient endurance and faithfulness" during a time of severe trial so that many others can come to follow Jesus. But God's justice will not be delayed forever. Having reviewed the historical developments leading up to the present crisis with the cult of emperor worship, the book of Revelation now looks to the future and depicts how the great empire that's persecuting God's people will be judged and destroyed. Three scenes challenge and encourage followers of Jesus not to receive "the mark of the beast." And then seven angels pour out "bowls of God's wrath" on the kingdom of the beast. This is the third series of seven divine judgments in the book.

READING

Have three different people read these scenes that lead up to the seven bowls:

 The Lamb and the 144,000 (beginning, "Then I looked, and there before me was the Lamb . . .")

The proclamations from heaven ("Then I saw another angel flying in midair . . .")

 The harvest of the earth ("I looked, and there before me was a white cloud . . .")

Then have someone read the introduction to the seven bowls (beginning, "I saw in heaven another great and marvelous sign . . .")

Finally, have different people take turns reading what happens as each of the seven bowls is poured out.

DISCUSSION

1 The "Lamb, standing on Mount Zion" contrasts directly with the second beast in the preceding scene, who has "two horns like a lamb" and forces people to worship the first beast. The 144,000 with the Lamb's name on their foreheads contrast directly with the people who have the name of the beast written on their foreheads. These images are juxtaposed to show that, despite deadly persecution, the cult of emperor worship will never stamp out the community of Jesus' followers. A great number of people will suffer and even die rather than worship anyone but the "Lamb who was slain" as their Savior. This scene is meant to encourage believers to stay faithful, even under great pressure. They're not alone: many others are staying faithful with them.

⟳ Do you ever feel alone in your faith, as if you're the only one who's still trying to follow Jesus, while others are compromising or giving up altogether? Take a few minutes to think of some people whose faithful commitment to Jesus, despite struggles and trials, is an encouragement to you. Tell the group about one of them if you can, and send this person a note, e-mail, or text message this week to thank them for their example.

⊃ Might your own faith and example be encouraging some people to follow Jesus, without you always being aware of it? If so, who might those people be? Take a moment to think about it.

2 While the first scene, of the Lamb and the 144,000, provides positive encouragement to keep following Jesus, the second scene, of the angels flying through the air, warns of the negative consequences of worshipping the emperor. Anyone who does is giving their allegiance to an empire that's doomed, and they'll perish with it.

In an allusion to earlier prophetic books, Rome is called "Babylon the Great." The empire that took God's people captive in Daniel's time serves as a symbol for the empire that's persecuting them in John's day. And like Babylon, which was destroyed because of its arrogance and oppression, Rome, too, will be destroyed. (This image of the "fall of Babylon" will be developed in more detail in the next section of Revelation.)

⊃ What kinds of things in your culture that are contrary to God's purposes compete for the loyalty and allegiance of those who want to follow Jesus? What can help us see them in an eternal perspective, as things that are doomed to perish, along with any investment we make in them?

3 The image of the winepress provides one more incentive for followers of Jesus to stay faithful to him. The time when God will judge and punish their persecutors is coming very soon: "the time to reap has come, for the harvest of the earth is ripe." (This image is another of the Scriptural symbols used in the book of Revelation. It comes from the end of the book of Joel, where it's used as a description of definitive judgment: "Swing the sickle, for the harvest is ripe. Come, trample the grapes, for the winepress is full and the vats overflow—so great is their wickedness!")

⊃ God is always working to bring his purposes for our lives to the point where they're "ripe" and come to fruition. If you've been waiting a long time for God to fulfill a specific purpose in your life (for example, to deliver you from trial or temptation, like the people in Revelation, or to bring about some other kind of breakthrough), what signs of progress can you identify, in yourself and in your circumstances, that suggest this time of "ripeness" might be approaching?

4 The series of seven bowls is similar to the series of seals and trumpets. Once again the first four judgments are directed against four parts of creation. Like the trumpets, the bowls release plagues like the ones that God sent against Pharaoh in Egypt: sores, waters turned to blood, darkness, a great thunderstorm with hailstones, and frogs (although these frogs are "demonic spirits"). And like the sixth trumpet, the sixth bowl opens the way to armies from the east of the Euphrates River, foreshadowing the barbarian invasions that will eventually overwhelm Rome. But this time, there's no interlude between the sixth and seventh bowls. The "hour of [God's] judgment has come," and the series culminates immediately in the destruction of the "great city" by a devastating earthquake, symbolizing the fall of Rome.

As God sends plagues to destroy the kingdom of the beast, he's praised in three different songs for his divine quality of justice: "just and true are your ways . . . your righteous acts have been revealed"; "you are just in these judgments"; "true and just are your judgments." God makes sure that those who definitively refuse to repent experience the consequences. This, the songs are saying, is an admirable and praiseworthy aspect of God's character. It's not revenge. It's justice.

⊃ Working alone or with others in your group, write a prayer thanking God for his justice. You might recall times in your own life when God let you learn a lesson the hard way, when you wouldn't learn it any other way. You might thank God for how people, great and small, have been caught and held accountable for doing wrong or abusing their positions. Also pray for God's justice to be carried out in the world today, to set people free from hardened oppressors. Those who wish can read all or part of their prayers out loud to the group, and everyone can say "Amen" together at the end of each one.

"IN THE SPIRIT"
IN THE WILDERNESS

THE FALL OF "BABYLON THE GREAT"

INTRODUCTION

The fall of Rome ("Babylon the Great") has been announced; the book of Revelation now zooms in on this event to depict it in more detail. This depiction forms a distinct section within the book. It's marked off at its beginning and end by interactions that John has with one of the angels who had the seven bowls. John says once again that he's "in the Spirit," meaning he's receiving a new vision, this time in "a wilderness." (His long vision of heavenly worship and divine judgments will conclude after this section.)

This vision of the "fall of Babylon" makes the audacious claim that Rome, then at the height of its power, will collapse. Rome will be judged for its emperor worship, and for its persecution of God's people, but also for its addiction to luxury and self-indulgence and how this has affected the rest of the world. This section of the book has much to say to people who live in powerful and affluent countries.

READING

Have two people in your group read the description and interpretation of John's vision of the "great prostitute." One can be the narrator and speak in John's voice as he describes what he sees; the other can take the part of the angel and read what he says.

In the rest of this section, a variety of characters sing songs about "Babylon." Some of these songs are laments (songs of mourning), but others are taunts (saying the city has gotten what it deserves). Have the members of your group take turns reading the songs of each of the following characters, including their narrative introductions:

Angel from heaven
Another voice from heaven
Kings of the earth
Merchants of the earth
Sea captains and sailors
Mighty angel
Great multitude
Elders and living creatures
Voice from the throne
Great multitude

Finally, have the same two people who portrayed John and the angel read the conclusion to this section (beginning, "Then the angel said to me" and ending, "For the testimony of Jesus is the Spirit of prophecy").

DISCUSSION

1 In the first part of this section, Rome is depicted as a "great prostitute." This is a literal reference to the city's immorality, and a figurative reference, using a common Scriptural motif, to its idolatry. The details of the portrait are intended to identify the guilty city and emperor.

Some details are transparent. John's audience would have clearly understood "the great city that rules over the kings of the earth" to mean Rome. The famous "seven hills" that the city sits on reinforce this identification. Other details can be understood in light of the symbolism in Revelation and its Scriptural background. The "beast" that "once was, now is not, and will come up out of the Abyss and go to its destruction" is likely a depiction of the spirit of Nero that has come back to life in the person of Domitian. The emperor's pretensions to divinity are being parodied by contrast to the true God, who "was, and is, and is to come." The "ten horns" are explained as "ten kings," likely symbolizing all of the rulers under Rome's authority (ten being a number of completeness). At first these rulers will be loyal to Rome, but they will then turn against the city and help destroy it, as depicted in this vision. They'll do this under the influence of the "beast," the spirit of empire gone bad, who to this point has been the force behind Rome and its persecuting emperor, but who will abandon the city in the end. The beast itself will be destroyed when Jesus "judges" it "with justice," as we'll see in the next session.

The biggest puzzle in the portrait is the identity of the "seven heads" that represent "seven kings." As he did for the number of the beast, John says that this "calls for a mind with wisdom," meaning that there's some kind of twist to the puzzle—some key to how the kings (apparently Roman emperors) are being counted. Unfortunately, a straightforward solution to this puzzle has not yet been identified; interpreters offer a variety of explanations. But in some way John is trying to portray the persecuting emperor as the culmination of imperial arrogance (seven being a number of totality), which then takes a further step into satanic evil as the emperor becomes "the beast," "an eighth king."

In whatever way its individual details are interpreted, the vulgar image of the "great prostitute" reveals that Rome, despite its wealth, splendor, and pretensions, has been corrupting the world and is "drunk with the blood of God's people." It fully deserves the judgment it's about to receive.

⊃ A political cartoon depicts the Statue of Liberty in a halter top, short skirt, and high heels leaning over into the ships entering New York harbor and saying, "Hi, honey, looking for a date?" In the background are images of an adult video storefront, risky financial investments, high energy consumption, the arms trade, etc. What is this cartoon trying to say? What would you say in response?

2 In the rest of this section, taunts and laments trace the downfall of "Babylon the Great." (They draw on the language and imagery of Ezekiel, who describes merchants mourning for the city of Tyre, and Jeremiah, who describes the downfall of the original Babylon.) While Rome is punished for oppression and idolatry, it's also condemned for destructive indulgence and excessive consumption: "Give her as much torment and grief as the glory and luxury she gave herself." As depicted here, merchants brought luxury goods to Rome from around the world, and the list of these goods tells a story of greed, excess, waste, and exploitation. For example:

- Rome practiced such excesses that its women would bathe in tubs made of silver, but gold and silver were mined by slaves doing forced labor under inhumane conditions
- the purple dye described here was made from the blood of a shellfish; in some coastal villages, half the population would sit all day draining this blood out, one drop at a time
- elephants in great numbers were hunted and killed for their ivory
- the wood at the bottom of Thyine trees ("costly wood") could produce spectacular designs, so entire trees were toppled, their bottoms were sliced off, and everything else was left to rot.

In short, Rome's luxury trade shaped the economy of its world, fueling consumption, wasting human potential, and despoiling natural resources. God announced his judgment against the city just as much for this as for its idolatry and immorality.

⟳ This section of Revelation suggests that luxury and overconsumption are contrary to God's purposes for human life and culture, and that practicing moderation and simplicity is vital to our spiritual lives. What practical steps have you taken, or can you take, in each of the following areas?

- cultivating a lifestyle of simplicity
- caring for the environment
- reducing energy use
- not depriving other people of their heritage in nature and culture
- helping people find meaningful, creative work

➲ As a group project, have everyone go through their closets and cupboards this week and pull out surplus clothes and household items that are in good condition. Bring them all to your next meeting, and choose a couple of members to deliver them to a charity thrift store in your community. Have them give a report about the delivery at the following meeting.

NOTE

At the end of this section, characters we've met earlier, like the elders and living creatures, and some we'll meet later, like the "bride," praise God for bringing his purposes in history to their culmination. This is an anticipation of the vision of the New Jerusalem, the last section of the book of Revelation. The symbolism and themes introduced at the end of this session's reading will be developed more fully in that section, when John is "in the Spirit" on a mountain.

"IN THE SPIRIT"
IN HEAVEN, CONTINUED

DEFEAT OF GOD'S ENEMIES, FINAL JUDGMENT, AND RENEWED CREATION

Book of Revelation > "In the Spirit" in Heaven > Conclusion

(At this meeting, choose a couple of members to deliver the second-hand clothes and household items your group has collected to a thrift store in your community. Have them report back at your next meeting.)

INTRODUCTION

An angel took John aside to show him the "punishment of the great prostitute," but John now steps back into his heavenly vision (saying, as he did at the start, "I saw heaven standing open"). He witnesses the outcome of the conflict with the dragon and the beasts in a series of scenes that brings this long vision to a close.

In these scenes, the vision shifts to the more distant future, as happened at the end of Daniel. It becomes harder to correlate details with known historical events. Things are depicted that clearly have not yet happened, such as Christ's return, the resurrection, the final judgment, and the renewal of heaven and earth. As we've noted, a similar shift in focus, from the more immediate future to the more distant future, also occurs in other biblical visions and prophecies, as a definitive crisis in the life of God's people evokes the ultimate crisis at the end of this age. So these final scenes in the heavenly vision give us a tantalizing but hazy glimpse into the final outworking of God's purposes for human history.

READING

Have four people read these scenes out loud for the rest of the group:

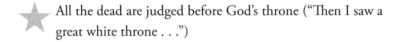 The "rider on the horse" fights against the beast and his army (beginning, "I saw heaven standing open and there before me was a white horse . . .")

The dragon is imprisoned for a thousand years, but then leads another revolt ("And I saw an angel coming down out of heaven, having the key to the Abyss . . .")

All the dead are judged before God's throne ("Then I saw a great white throne . . .")

A new world appears, where God will live with people (beginning, "Then I saw 'a new heaven and a new earth' . . ." and ending, "This is the second death.")

DISCUSSION

1 John has foreseen that Rome will be destroyed as "the beast and the kings of the earth" turn against the empire. But the beast remains a threat to the followers of Jesus. Until he and his false prophet are defeated, they can continue to "delude" the nations into worshipping false gods and persecuting those who won't. So Jesus comes with the "armies of heaven" to battle against these enemies.

The portrait of Jesus, and of the battle, is once again painted with symbols drawn from the Scriptures. Most have been used earlier in the book. Many come from the opening vision (Jesus is "Faithful and True," he has eyes "like blazing fire," a "sharp sword" comes out of his mouth) and from the promises made in the letters to "those who are victorious" (Jesus has a secret name, he's dressed in white). Others come from later visions in the book ("he will rule them with an iron scepter," he "treads the winepress of the fury of the wrath of God"). Some symbols are drawn directly from other Scriptures: The "robe dipped in blood" is a figure from the end of Isaiah; summoning the birds to the "great supper of God" evokes one of Ezekiel's visions.

The symbolic nature of this vision is seen most clearly at its end, when the "armies gathered together" are killed by the "sword coming out of the mouth of the rider on the horse." Clearly this war is not being described literally. Rather, this is a symbolic depiction of the return of Jesus to defeat the forces of deception and idolatry that have been turned loose in the Roman world.

From our historical vantage point two thousand years later, we know that Jesus' actual return did not take place in these times. But John portrays it, from his perspective, as if it would happen shortly after the other events described in the book. This phenomenon is known as "prophetic foreshortening." It's like looking over a mountain ridge and seeing another mountain beyond it, but not all of the hills and valleys that lie in between. However, even if Jesus' actual return was delayed, the "word of God" (symbolized by the sword) did defeat the enemies of Jesus' followers in these days.

⮑ In which of the following forms do you think the "word of God" is most active in the world today? How is the word of God in this form bringing about transformation?

   a. The Scriptures, as they're read, studied, taught, and preached in the community of Jesus' followers.

   b. The person of Jesus, who's in relationship with his followers and reaching out personally to people around the world.

   c. The social witness of Jesus' followers, as they "speak truth to power" through word and deed.

   d. Inspired words spoken by modern-day prophets to the church and the world.

   e. Some other form.

2 John foresees that the fall of Rome and the defeat of idolatry will give the followers of Jesus an extended season of peace, symbolized here as 1,000 years (10 x 10 x 10). During this time those who gave their lives for their faith in Jesus will begin to enjoy their reward in his presence. But John also foresees that a new threat will one day arise from the "nations in the four corners of the earth"—peoples living outside the empire. These distant nations may be led astray in the future, just as Rome was. John envisions a climactic battle at the end of history as the devil gathers the nations of the world to attack "the camp of God's people." (The scene once again draws on the imagery of Ezekiel: His prince "Gog, of the land of Magog" becomes "Gog and Magog," a rhyming phrase to describe this horde of nations.) The attacking army is destroyed by fire from heaven, and the devil is definitively judged and punished.

⮑ The idea of a "millennium" or thousand-year reign of Christ has been an inspiration to followers of Jesus throughout the ages. Many have expected a period of universal peace and justice to arrive on earth through social reform, education, and reconciliation efforts spearheaded by Jesus' followers. (This expectation fueled crusades for public education, the abolition of slavery, the vote for women, temperance, pacifism, an end to child labor, etc.) Others have held that only the Second Coming of Christ could definitively bring about such a period. And still others have understood the millennium spiritually, as a picture of Christ's reign in heaven and in the hearts of believers. Which of these views is closest to your understanding? (If you've never thought about this before, take some time to decide.) What positive value do you see in the other views? What "action steps" does each of these views call for?

3 The book of Revelation now depicts the final judgment, in symbolism drawn from Daniel's vision of the Ancient of Days ("thrones were set in place, and the Ancient of Days took his seat . . . The court was seated, and the books were opened"). Everyone who has ever lived is held accountable for what they've done. Those whose names are not written in the "book of life" experience a "second death" as they're "thrown into the lake of fire."

The "book of life," which records the names of those who belong to God, is an image found in Daniel's fourth vision ("everyone whose name is found written in the book will be delivered") and several other places in the Bible.

Luke, for example, records that Jesus told his followers to "rejoice that your names are written in heaven."

⮑ How does a person's name come to be written in the "book of life" (speaking of the reality behind this symbol)? Do you have confidence that your name is written there? If not, speak with some members of your group who do have this confidence, and ask them why they have it.

⮑ It's impossible for a literal fire to burn a finite amount of fuel forever. So the image of the "lake of fire" can't be taken to mean that people who've definitively rejected a relationship with God, and who have lived destructively in opposition to God's purposes, will literally and physically "burn up forever." What reality do you think this symbol is pointing to? (There's a suggested answer you can interact with at the end of this session.)

4 The long vision that fills most of the book of Revelation concludes with a description of a "new heaven and a new earth" and "the new Jerusalem coming down out of heaven." (The final section of the book, when John is "in the Spirit" on a mountain, will zoom in on the new Jerusalem and symbolically explore its spiritual character, just as the true character of Rome was exposed in the vision John had when he was "in the Spirit" in the wilderness.) In the renewed creation, God dwells directly with people, and there's no suffering or pain. Every desire is satisfied in relationship with God himself ("to the thirsty I will give water without cost from the spring of the water of life"). John gives one more warning to his readers, who are being pressured to compromise with emperor worship, that all of these rewards are for "those who are victorious," not for the "cowardly" and "unbelieving" (or "unfaithful") who abandon Jesus and become part of the oppressive evil around them.

⮑ What do you look forward to most when you picture God dwelling directly among people?

NOTE

Suggested answer to section 3, question 2: The image of the "lake of fire" symbolizes, at least, that people who definitively reject God will be separated permanently from him, they will always be objects of his displeasure, and they will never receive the comfort and satisfaction that God gives those who do live in his presence. There's a further discussion of this question in the next session.

FOR YOUR NEXT MEETING

Make sure that internet access, or a good dictionary, is available to the group to look up some specialized terms.

If you have an artist in your group, ask them to bring their art supplies the next time so they can do a color illustration.

"IN THE SPIRIT"
ON A MOUNTAIN

THE NEW JERUSALEM

Book of Revelation > "In the Spirit" on a Mountain
Book of Revelation > Epilogue

INTRODUCTION

John's final vision in the book of Revelation is of "the Holy City, the new Jerusalem, coming down out of heaven." This is the fourth major section within the book. John says once more that he's "in the Spirit," having a new vision, this time from a "mountain great and high." An angel gives him a tour of the city and he witnesses its grandeur, glory, and grace.

The book then closes by reviewing the purposes it announced in its prologue. It says again that God has "sent his angel to show his servants the things that must soon take place." In an epilogue, John names himself as the one who received these visions, just as he did in the prologue. Jesus is again identified by many titles, to authenticate the revelation he has given. John warns his readers not to add anything to his words or to take anything from them. And just as the book began like a letter, it ends the way a letter of the time would have ended, with a "grace wish": "The grace of the Lord Jesus be with God's people. Amen."

READING

Have one person read the description of the new Jerusalem. Everyone else should close their eyes and try to picture what's being described.

Then have someone read the epilogue to the book of Revelation (beginning, "I, John, am the one who heard and saw these things").

DISCUSSION

1 The new Jerusalem is described symbolically to portray the glories and perfections of a place where God will dwell personally with his people. It's depicted as a cube, a perfectly symmetrical shape, with symbolic dimensions: each side is 12 x 10 x 10 x 10 stadia long, and the wall is 12 x 12 cubits thick. The number 12, emblematic of the community that lives in relationship with God, is used in several other ways to fill out the portrait. The city has 12 gates, made of 12 pearls, with 12 angels and the names of the 12 tribes; it has 12 foundations made of 12 precious stones with the names of the 12 apostles. The tree of life bears 12 crops each year. Dazzling gold and precious stones adorn the city's foundations, gates, and streets, and it's lit up by the very glory of God.

> ⟳ If your group has internet access, work together to search for the names of the precious stones listed here. (If you don't have internet access, you can pass around a dictionary and have people take turns looking up the names.) What colors are they? Which are translucent, and which are opaque? What would the city look like if there were three precious-stone foundations on each of its four sides? If someone in your group has brought art supplies, have them sketch or paint the scene in color. What does this picture communicate to you?

⊃ What do you think it would be like to live in this city? What would be the biggest differences from where you live now?

2 At the end of the main vision in the book of Revelation, all those whose names are not written in the book of life—the cowardly, unbelieving, vile, murderers, sexually immoral, those who practice magic arts, idolaters, and liars—are thrown into the "lake of fire." In this vision, we're told that "only those whose names are written in the Lamb's book of life" may enter the city; "outside" are "those who practice magic arts, the sexually immoral, murderers, idolaters" and liars. If these same people have already been thrown into the lake of fire, why do they need to be denied entrance to this city?

The details of these two visions can't be reconciled by a literal reading, but this only shows that both are meant to be understood symbolically. In this part of the Jerusalem vision, John is drawing on language and imagery from the end of book of Isaiah, where the restored Jerusalem is told:

> Your gates will always stand open,
>> they will never be shut, day or night,
> so that people may bring you the wealth of the nations—
>> their kings led in triumphal procession . . .
> The sun will no more be your light by day,
>> nor will the brightness of the moon shine on you,
> for the LORD will be your everlasting light,
>> and your God will be your glory.

So two different figures are used—being thrown in the lake of fire and being denied entrance to the city where God lives with his people. But their message is the same: those who definitively reject God will be kept out of his presence, while those who remain loyal and faithful, even through sacrifice and suffering, will live forever with God in a place of splendor and glory.

⊃ Now that you've read and discussed the entire book of Revelation, what would you say are the essential things it discloses to us about God's purposes for the culmination of human history? What can we know with a high degree of certainty, and what things do we have to be more tentative about? Has your perspective on this changed over the course of these sessions?

3 There are several parallels between this depiction of the new Jerusalem and the depiction of "Babylon the Great." At the start of each of these distinct visions within the book, one of the angels who had the seven bowls says to John, "Come, I will show you . . . ," and then zooms in on a city that's already been described in the main vision. At the end of each depiction, John falls down to worship this angel, but he's told, "Don't do that! I am a fellow servant . . . Worship God!" Each city is symbolized by a woman. But these parallel portraits are designed to create a contrast. Babylon is the "great prostitute," while the new Jerusalem is "a bride beautifully dressed for her husband." Babylon is "fallen," while Jerusalem is "coming down out of heaven from God." The two contrasting images are displayed together to show readers that there's no middle ground: They're living in either one city or the other.

➲ Do you approach your life as if there's plenty of middle ground between giving your allegiance to the evil, oppressive forces in the world, and making a total commitment to follow Jesus? If there really isn't any middle ground, which side are you on?

4 The book of Revelation concludes with double calls to "come." The Spirit and the bride call to "those who are thirsty" to come and "take the free gift of the water of life." All who have heard the book read aloud are asked to join in extending this invitation. And when Jesus declares, "Yes, I am coming soon," John replies, "Amen. Come, Lord Jesus."

➲ Invite anyone in your group who hasn't yet received the "free gift of the water of life" to accept this gift from God. Pray together with anyone who wants to receive it.

➲ Conclude your study of Revelation by having someone read Jesus' statement, "Yes, I am coming soon," and having everyone reply together, "Amen. Come, Lord Jesus."

 The Books of The Bible

Clean. Beautiful. Unshackled.

- chapter and verse numbers removed
  (chapter and verse range given at bottom of page)
- natural literary breaks
- no additives: notes, cross-references,
  and section headings removed
- single-column setting
- whole books restored (Luke-Acts)
- book order provides greater help in understanding

There is no Bible more suited to reading—from the beginning of the book to the end—than *The Books of The Bible*. This "new" approach is actually the original approach, and I love it.

Scot McKnight
North Park University

For more information or to download the gospel of John, visit http://www.thebooksofthebible.info. Premium editions of this Bible will be available in Spring 2011 from Zondervan at your favorite Christian retailer.

ALSO AVAILABLE

Bible reading is declining at such a rapid rate that within 30 years the Bible will be a "thing of the past" for most Christ-followers. One of the main reasons for this decline is the format of the Bible. The format we know today was created so that a "modern" world could divide and analyze and systematize the Scriptures. But this made the word of God practically unreadable. As we move into a postmodern world, we'll need to recapture the stories, songs, poems, letters, and dreams that naturally fill the pages of Scripture. Only then will a new generation of readers return to the Bible.

Christopher Smith argues in this book that the "time for chapters and verses is over." He explains how these divisions of the biblical text interfere with our reading and keep us from understanding the Scriptures. He describes how Biblica has created a new format for the Bible, without chapters and verses, with the biblical books presented in their natural forms. And he shares the exciting new approaches people are already taking to reading, studying, preaching, and teaching the Bible in this new presentation.

Paperback, 234 pages, 5.5 x 8.5
ISBN: 978-1-60657-044-9
Retail: $15.99

Available for purchase online or through your local bookstore.

7/3/13

3/23/18 - not much underlined